Pennsylvania Mountain Vistas

A Guide for Hikers and Photographers

Scott E. Brown

STACKPOLE
BOOKS

To the Keystone Trails Association,
their affiliated hiking clubs,
and all the people who lovingly maintain
thousands of miles of trails in
Penn's Woods, thank you.

Copyright ©2007 by Stackpole Books

Published by
STACKPOLE BOOKS
5067 Ritter Road
Mechanicsburg, PA 17055
www.stackpolebooks.com

Printed in China

10 9 8 7 6 5 4 3 2 1

FIRST EDITION

Design by Beth Oberholtzer
Cover design by Caroline Stover

Cover: Canyon Vista, Wyoming State Forest
Back cover: Sunrise at The Throne Room, Rothrock State Forest

Library of Congress Cataloging-in-Publication Data

Brown, Scott E., 1962–
    Pennsylvania mountain vistas : a guide for hikers and photographers /
Scott E. Brown.– 1st ed.
        p.   cm.
      ISBN-13: 978-0-8117-3439-4 (pbk. : alk. paper)
      ISBN-10: 0-8117-3439-0 (pbk. : alk. paper)
      1. Hiking–Pennsylvania–Guidebooks.   2. Outdoor photography–
Pennsylvania–Guidebooks.   3. Pennsylvania–Guidebooks.   I. Title.

GV199.42.P4B758   2008
796.5109748–dc22
                                                                2007009817

Contents

Introduction

Everyone who hikes ends up at a mountain view, scenic overlook, or vista at some point, even if it's just on a short outing close to home. Why we hike to high places is different for each of us. For some, it's the exercise and effort involved, a desire to feel the burn from God's own Stairmaster. Others may seek escape from the office grind for several hours. Sometimes it's simply to get a kind of payoff for one's time.

I think most of us, however, hike to a magnificent view because we seek inspiration. We wish to be in awe of nature's handiwork, and that's what this book is about: a passion to seek high places and exhilarating locales. As one of my T-shirts says "Seek the road less traveled. . . . On second thought forget the road."

So please, throw on a pair of boots and seek the road less traveled, because at the end is a magnificent view.

Safety

I would be remiss if I didn't begin by talking about safety with this stern warning: You are solely responsible for your own safety.

Heights

The wonderful thing about shooting from high places is the unique view of the world, but the downside is that a stumble is no minor thing. You'd be surprised how a short fall can get you seriously hurt. In short, people don't bounce.

Working from high places can also be tricky on the mind. I've hung my toes off 2,000-foot cliffs in Utah and felt fine, yet I've become a bit funky standing on a ladder to change a lightbulb. Here's the point: No matter how comfortable you are with heights, you never know when a feeling of vertigo might hit. If you do feel dizzy, don't try to sit, but simply kneel down and put one hand down to create a tripodlike posture. Stability is king when you get lightheaded.

Another issue to deal with is loose rock. Just because it looks solid doesn't mean it is. Generally speaking, the rocks in Pennsylvania cliffs are very hard and don't crack easily. But they are subject to frost wedging, so large slabs can peel away from a cliff at an inopportune moment. Check cliff edges by extending a tripod leg and poking at them good and hard. Then give them a good stomp. You're not checking to see if rocks will break free—you're listening for a hollow sound, like that of cracked stucco or plaster. If a rock slab has a hollow sound, it's no good to stand on. Find another spot.

Enormous boulders can shift without warning. While doing some work for Hawk Mountain Sanctuary, I was shooting at a place called The Cobbles, which is closed to the public. I stood on a rock the size of my truck, took a step, and it started to seesaw, which is an unnerving experience. If a boulder moves, step back and let it stabilize, then find another rock. Never forget, an object in motion will tend to stay in motion. Inertia, as Newton noted, has a funny habit of getting its way.

Lightning

Some of the most remarkable photographic light imaginable is found when the weather is changing radically. Seeking spectacular light is what photographers do, and amazing cloud formations tend to precede or follow violent weather. Remember the whole "red sky at night" saying? But the downside to seeking good cloud formations is lightning.

Being stuck on a mountain in a lightning storm is potentially deadly. The only way to protect yourself is to avoid getting caught. Always check the weather before a hike, and never hike when the forecast has a high probability of thunderstorms. Between May and October, thunderstorms can pop up without warning, especially in the mountains. I use a combination of local radio, weather.com, and intellicast.com to make my hiking decisions. Even so, I've been caught on ridges in lightning a number of times, and let's just say that such occasions provide a unique focus and motivation to seek safety.

The National Outdoor Leadership School (NOLS) and the National Weather Service Lightning Safety Office have a lot to say about lightning safety. NOLS's John Gookin has written a marvelous article on lightning safety, myths, and science that you can find online. Here are some tips based on his advice:

- Do not put yourself into a position where lightning can become a hazard. In short, do not hike if the forecast is for bad weather.

- If you can see it, flee it. If you can hear it, clear it. If you see lightning or hear thunder, leave the area and seek cover. The best possible cover is an enclosed modern building or other structure. The next best thing is a car, making sure not to touch any metallic surfaces inside the vehicle. Caves of any type are *not* considered good cover.

- Use the 30-30 rule: If the time delay between a lightning flash and the bang is thirty seconds or less, seek shelter immediately. Do not leave the shelter

Michael Keeler shows how to create the smallest possible target while minimizing contact with the ground. If you get caught by lightning, this is the position of last resort.

until it's been thirty minutes since you heard the last thunder. To calculate the distance to a lightning strike, take the time delay between flash and bang in seconds and divide by 5. A thirty-second delay means a strike is 6 miles away. It's common for thunderstorms to move at 30 miles per hour, so a strike 6 miles away gives you about twelve minutes to seek cover. That's not a lot of time.

- If you are caught in the open and cannot reach a building or vehicle, do the following:
  — Quickly get as far off the ridge as possible, descending as low as you can. Seek a ravine or other depression if possible.
  — Stay away from isolated trees; towers, power lines, or fences of any type; or anything metallic.
  — Drop your equipment and lay down your tripod. Stay a good distance away from both.
  — Individuals in groups should disperse as far from each other as practical; 50 feet of separation is a minimum distance.
  — Don't be the tallest thing around. Assume "lightning position," crouching in a tight ball with your feet together, and staying on the balls of your feet.

Cold Weather

Getting into the woods after a snowstorm is easier than you might think, and no, you don't need snowshoes, although they do help. Cold weather, in general, and snow, in particular, present a unique set of circumstances that hikers and photographers have to deal with. Cold fingers and chilly feet are the norm for the winter photographer, but hypothermia can set in without your realizing it, so it's important to know the warning signs:

- Shivering that may be controlled with activity is risky, but uncontrolled shivering is serious.
- Hands or feet that become stiff or moving joints that become painful when muscles tense.
- A feeling of fatigue or weakness.
- Skin that looks waxy or pale or feels numb when touched.

If you have any of these warning signs, get out of the cold as quickly as you can. Here's the thing, though: You're not always the best judge of how you feel. It's always a good idea to hike with a buddy in cold weather.

Frostbite is a threat to exposed skin even when it's not windy. Here are some warning signs:

- Skin that becomes white and is hard and cold to the touch.
- Pain or a burning sensation.
- Itching like you have a rash.
- Loss of feeling in the affected area.
- Mottled skin color.
- Skin that becomes red and blotchy when warmed, like a burn.

Even though cold-weather hiking presents some dangers, you can enjoy it by preparing carefully. The key is understanding how to dress. Here are some things to consider:

- Dress in many layers.
- Use synthetic fabrics designed to move moisture away from the skin. Avoid cotton, which will suck heat away from the body if it becomes wet.
- Wear a good hat and keep your ears covered.
- Wear mittens and thin synthetic glove liners.

The main point to consider is sweating and cooling cycles. While hiking, you'll sweat a lot, but when you stop at a location, you'll quickly get cold. For temperatures around 0°F, here's how I dress. I don a pair of wicking long johns covered by hiking pants and then rain pants. I use two or three pairs of socks, beginning with a wicking sock followed by pairs of heavy Smart-Wool. I wear leg gators and make sure my rain pants are tight around the ankles to keep snow out of my boots. On the upper body, I wear two wicking T-shirts followed by two long-sleeve shirts of increasing thickness. Over this I wear either a fleece vest or jacket topped with a good winter coat or a raincoat as a wind layer. To protect my hands, I use a thin pair of glove liners and high-quality convertible mittens made by Thinsulate. These fingerless gloves have a mitten-like flap that covers the fingers but can be folded back, keeping my hands nice and toasty while allowing me to use my fingers. I wear a good knit hat and a neck gator, and I take along one or two bandannas and a pair of ear muffs called 180s.

While hiking, remove layers when you begin to sweat. It's not uncommon for me to peel down to my inner layers and wear only a head bandanna at 10°F. Trouble can start when you get to a location and stop moving. Don't wait to cool off before relayering. Immediately put on everything you have, especially a cap. Once you get to a vista, you may not move much again for an hour or more. Good socks and boots mean everything when you're standing still. Never buy inexpensive cold-weather clothing, especially boots. Seek a good outfitter and ask lots of questions.

When it comes to winter fitness, you need to know your limits. You'll exert yourself much more in snow than you anticipate. When there's a foot of snow on the ground, trail difficulties increase—an easy hike becomes difficult and a difficult hike even more so. Unseen rocks will have a thin layer of ice on them, so you're not just walking against greater resistance, you're walking on big slippery marbles as well. Don't fear exploring the winter landscape, just start small.

Winter hiking can also be hard on your camera equipment. Fine, powdery snow blows around easily in the calmest breeze and gets into everything unless care is taken. Here are some pointers:

- Keep your camera bag closed as much as possible. It doesn't need to be zipped tight; just keep your gear covered.
- Stand up to change lenses, using a coat as a windbreak.
- If you drop something in the snow, *don't blow on it in order to clean it.* Hot breath will only make matters worse. Use canned air, a squeeze ball, or a sable-hair brush to remove snow from equipment.
- Allow your equipment to acclimatize by keeping it in the cold before you shoot. This is easily done by locking it in your car overnight, if you think it's going to be safe.
- When bringing in gear from the cold, put camera bodies and lenses in freezer bags before entering a warm room. This way condensation or frost will form on the bag and not inside an expensive camera. In fact, don't even open the camera bag for a couple hours after coming in, just in case.
- Modern electronic cameras, especially digital equipment, will eat batteries in cold weather. Always carry extra batteries, and keep at least one set in a warm pocket. Make sure there are no coins in that pocket, since powerful batteries can short across loose change and burn you.

Hunting Season

Some of the best times to shoot are during hunting season. All but a handful in forest and park areas are closed to hunting, and many vistas are on state game lands. The State Game Commission recommends that everyone, not just hunters, wear 100 square inches of blaze orange above the waist year-round. I recommend an orange hat and putting lots of orange on your pack as well. Do everything you can to be easily seen during dusky lighting conditions. For a list of hunting seasons, check the Game Commission's website.

Night Hiking

Getting to a sunrise location or returning from a sunset requires hiking in the dark. Night hiking is a unique and, believe it or not, truly fun thing to do. If you've never hiked in the dark, there are some things to take into account beforehand. Perhaps the biggest is how different trails look in the dark and how little you can actually see. By headlamp, your view of the world is only a few feet wide, and at best you can see just a dozen yards ahead. Your color vision isn't reliable, and blazes are difficult to see, landmarks are hard to find and recognize, and drop-offs are almost invisible. Stumbling over rocks is an ever-present problem as well. Simply put, you just can't move as quickly as you can in daylight, so don't try.

Many of the trails in this guide are short in-and-out hikes with few trail intersections. Still, it's easy to walk off a trail in the dark, and finding it again can be difficult. Even when you've moved only a few yards, the trail you were just on can be invisible. Here are some tips on preparing for a night hike:

- Hike the route in daylight as a test.
- Carry a cell phone.
- Carry three forms of illumination. I use a headlamp along with a small flashlight clipped to my pack. I also keep a large flashlight in a pocket. Take along extra batteries for all.
- Move slowly and pause often. Alternate your gaze from your feet to the limit of your headlamp. Trails are easily lost when you only look down at your feet. Pause often, looking to the rear to see if the trail is behind you.
- Carry a good map, compass, and a GPS unit if you have it. Make sure to mark your vehicle position.
- Use trekking poles, which are a help in rocky terrain. If you don't have them, then keep your hands free in case you stumble.
- Stumbling and tripping are inevitable. Learn to fall down gracefully.
- Don't panic. If you lose the trail, take a moment to get your bearings. Then, as carefully as possible, backtrack your route, pausing often and moving just a few yards at a time. If you are completely lost, stay put and *don't panic!* Wait until daylight before attempting to hike out.

Something else to deal with is what can best be described as the willies. Hiking in the dark, especially for the first time, can cause you to imagine all manner of things lurking just out of view. I've often had deer jump in front of me, and every time it scares me to death. You just have to get used to it. In darkness, animals can see much better than you can, and they'll avoid you if possible.

Perhaps the one thing you'll encounter that taps into people's deepest psyche is bats. Bats scare most people more than any other creature you can name. Having them zip noiselessly past your head is the admission price for nocturnal hiking, so get used to the idea. Try not to scream, and don't worry—they're after the bugs that your sweat, breath, and headlamp attract.

I've found that having bats nearby affords a rare opportunity to observe them at close quarters, and I think they're very cool to have around.

Snakes also tend to freak people out. I encountered probably thirty timber rattlesnakes in creating this guide, all of them while hiking across rocks. Their rattling buzz is a unique sound that will get your attention—quickly. It's OK to scream and then jump a few feet out of the way. Typically a snake is only warning you it's there; simply divert several feet around it. Never harm any snake you encounter. Just let it be.

Ethics and Etiquette

Vista locations can be small, and the pressure to capture rapidly changing light intense. Many times I've seen amateur photographers arrive at a location and try to bully their way to a desirable position or simply set up in front of others. This is not acceptable behavior. Respect and common courtesy go a long way toward getting what you want. Words such as "please," "thank you," and "may I" work wonders—use them. In tight locations, ask if you can nest your tripod legs among others. Always ask permission before setting up in front of somebody else; then be quick and get out of the way.

Consider becoming a member of the North American Nature Photography Association. NANPA is a strong proponent of ethical behavior among nature photographers, and their ethics principle states:

> Every place, plant, and animal, whether above or below water, is unique, and cumulative impacts occur over time. Therefore one must always exercise good individual judgment. It is NANPA's belief that these principles will encourage all who participate in the enjoyment of nature to do so in a way that best promotes good stewardship of the resource.

To paraphrase some of NANPA's guidelines as they apply to photographing from vista points:

- Stay on trails that are intended to lessen impact.
- Do not cross, climb, or circumvent fences that are placed for your safety.
- When appropriate, inform resource managers or authorities of your presence and purpose.
- Learn the rules and laws of the location.
- In the absence of management authority, use good judgment.
- Prepare yourself and your equipment for unexpected events.
- Treat others courteously.
- Tactfully inform others if you observe them engaging in inappropriate or harmful behavior.
- Report inappropriate behavior. (Don't argue with those that don't care—report them.)

- Be a good role model, as both a photographer and a citizen. Don't interfere with the enjoyment of others.

I feel very strongly that we should conduct ourselves in the field by the guiding principle that the natural world is not an inheritance given to us by our elders, but a sacred trust we keep for our children and grandchildren. Perhaps the National Park Service sums it up best: "Take only pictures, leave only footprints."

How to Use this Guide

This guide divides the state into regions, and within each region, it groups vistas geographically. Generally speaking, where there's one vista, others will be nearby.

Driving distances are provided in miles, and road names, where they exist, are given along with the route numbers. The best map to have when using this guide is DeLorme's *Pennsylvania Gazetteer*. In addition, before venturing into state forests or game lands, obtain a copy of the relevant public use map.

Global Positioning System (GPS) coordinates for parking areas and vistas are given in degrees and decimal minutes. In many cases, the coordinates are from the U.S. Geologic Survey (USGS) Geospatial Information System database, known as GIS. National Geographic's *TOPO! State* series CD-ROM maps were used to get this information. These GIS coordinates were ground verified using a Garmin E-Trex handheld GPS unit. For vistas that have no USGS GIS location, the E-Trex was used to mark the location.

Round-trip hiking distances are in miles, and times are given as well. Hiking times are for daylight, snowfree conditions and based on a conservative combination of my hike time and Naismith's Rule (allow one hour for every three miles, and add an additional hour for every 2,000 feet of vertical ascent). Hiking times do not include the time needed to set up, compose, shoot, and break down camera equipment. When planning a hike, consider how long you may take to photograph, based on past experience. Some locations lend themselves to only one composition, whereas others afford many hours of fine shooting. Plan accordingly.

Elevation changes are given in feet from the parking area and are the total elevation gain or loss for the route provided. If you go up 1,000 feet, then descend 200 feet, the elevation gain will be given as 1,000 feet.

Hikes are rated as easy, moderate, difficult, or strenuous. This is a subjective rating system that combines elevation gain, steepness, and trail conditions into a general statement of what to expect. Hike difficulties are rated on the conservative side. A very fit twenty-five-year-old may think I'm a sissy for rating a trail as difficult, whereas what I call a moderate hike may be a real bear for someone who's sixty, overweight, and smokes. Take your degree of fitness and experience into account when using these ratings.

Words such as *opposite, turn,* and *return* as used in the directions are from the perspective of the hiker. For example, "Turn right and look for an enormous boulder" means turn toward your right. In many cases, to make sure there's no ambiguity, I use redundant notations such as "From this point, turn left (west) and walk for 2 miles."

Most Pennsylvania vistas can be photographed at any time of day during any season. Generally speaking, the best time of day for east-facing vistas is from thirty minutes before sunrise to one hour after. For west-facing views, it's from one hour before sunset to thirty minutes after. The best times of year are spring, during the latter portion of leaf-out; autumn, during peak color; and winter, when there is fresh snow cover. Good photographs can be made at any time of year after a large storm moves through. Dramatic lighting typically follows clearing storms, and incredible skies usually precede them, so keep an eye on the weather forecast and plan accordingly. I encourage you to try to shoot moonrise and moonset during a full moon. At least once a month, moonrise occurs within several minutes of sunset, and the same thing with moonset and sunrise. These are thrilling times to take photographs.

Ratings, Measurements, and Vista Types

Pennsylvania has hundreds of vista points, but not all of them inspire wonder. In fact, a great many are overgrown or just plain bad. There is no system or governing body that defines what a good vista is, but there are some obvious criteria, such as being high up and having a clear field of view. For the photographer, there are other things to look for before hauling gear to a location. I look for a clean foreground free of dead brush and make sure rocks have no graffiti. The middle ground must be clean and lush as well. There should be no clear-cuts or mines in view. A good vista should be inspiring and afford a large number of compositional possibilities. The best have a sublime quality that calls you back to them time and again. Vistas are rated on a 0 to 5 scale, where a 5 is a must-see location. I have attempted to include only the best our state has to offer, so there is nothing less than a 2 in this guide; in fact, there aren't many 3s either.

Certain measurements are important when selecting a shooting location. I've taken the following into account in compiling this guide:

Relief—The vertical distance from the edge of a vista to what's immediately below. For cliffs and ledges, the more the better. Ridges and hilltops may have no relief.

Elevation difference—The vertical distance to the nearest low point of terrain.

Axis—The principal direction of the view, given in degrees (45°) or compass direction (northeast).

Field of View—The width of the visual field, given in degrees from left to right (30° to 160°).

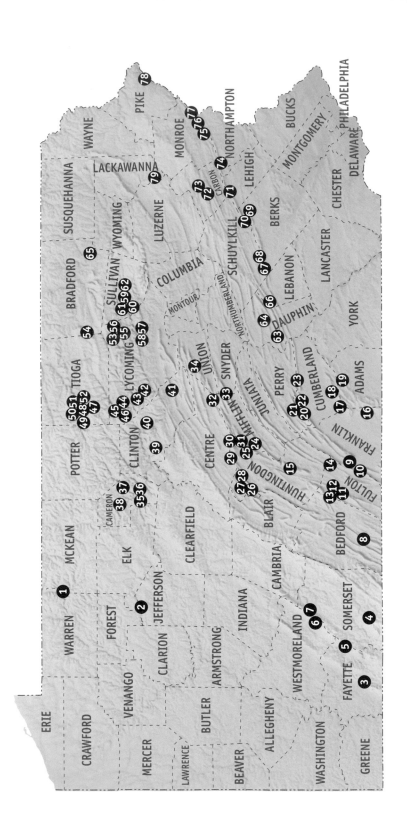

1. Rim Rock Overlook
2. Beartown Rocks
3. Pine Knob
4. Mount Davis High Point Tower
5. Laurel Hill
6. Wolf Rocks
7. Beam Rocks
8. Blankley Road
9. Tower Road
10. Tuscarora Summit Hang Glider Launch Site
11. Bark Road
12. Summit Road Hang Glider Launch Site
13. Fisher Road Hang Glider Launch Site
14. Priceless Point
15. The Throne Room
16. Chimney Rocks
17. Buzzard Rocks
18. Sunset Rocks
19. Pole Steeple
20. Three Square Hollow
21. Doubling Gap
22. Flat Rock
23. Waggoner's Gap Hawk Watch
24. Prayer Rock
25. Sausser's Stone Pile
26. Spruce Knob
27. Indian Overlook
28. The Promontory
29. Dave's Vista and Old Pine Vista
30. Indian Wells
31. Bear Meadows
32. Kohler and Long Mountains
33. New Lancaster Valley (Thick Mountain)
34. Shriner Mountain
35. Fred Woods Trail
36. Rocky Mountain Elk Foundation
37. Ives Farm
38. Whttimore Tower
39. Fish Dam Wild Area
40. Hyner View State Park
41. Ramm Road
42. Ramsey Road Overlook
43. Sinking Spring Overlook
44. Black Forest Trail
45. Hemlock Mountain
46. Ice Break Vista
47. Bradley Wales Picnic Area
48. Cushman Hollow
49. Elk Run
50. Colton Point State Park
51. Barbour Rock
52. Leonard Harrison State Park
53. Band Rock
54. Lambs View Picnic Area
55. Sharp Top
56. Old Loggers Path
57. Allegheny Ridge
58. Rider Park
59. Upper and Lower Alpine Views
60. Kettle Creek Gorge
61. High Knob Overlook
62. Canyon Vista
63. Table Rock
64. Weiser Hang Glider Launch Site
65. Wyalusing Rocks
66. Trout Run
67. Kimmel View and Fisher Lookout
68. Round Head
69. The Pinnacle and Pulpit Rock
70. Hawk Mountain
71. Bake Oven Knob
72. Lehigh Gorge West Side
73. Tank Hollow, Lehigh Gorge East Side
74. Delp Overlook
75. Wolf Rocks
76. Nelson Vista and Lunch Rocks
77. Delaware Water Gap
78. Tri State Rock and Cliff Park
79. Pine Knob Tower

Vistas also come in many types. The USGS recognizes a large number of names for different terrain features and high points. I've decided to use only the following four:

Cliff—Rock formation with large vertical relief where the terrain below falls away steeply. Typically cannot be climbed from below without special equipment and training.

Ledge—Rock formation with less vertical relief than a cliff, where the terrain does not fall away so steeply. Typically can be climbed from below without special equipment and training.

Cobble—A boulder field, boulder fall, talus slope, or patch of rock scree that forms an open area on a ridge crest or flank.

Ridge or summit—A location with no distinct edge that may or may not have vegetation cover.

Footgear and Equipment

Pennsylvania is known—perhaps infamous—for its rocky trails. Valley and Ridge Province trails such as the Appalachian Trail (AT) are quite rocky. In fact, there's an old saying about the AT: "Pennsylvania is where boots go to die." Although you can get most anywhere with a good pair of sneakers, I don't recommend them. Ankle and arch support are very important when hiking, especially when you need to do a lot of rock hopping, which you will, and stout, high-top boots are a must. A twisted ankle is a common hiking injury, and as I can attest, you can break an ankle anywhere, anytime. Stubbed toes are also very common. Make sure you have ample room for your toes, and keep the ankle laced tight.

Toting around 30 to 50 pounds of camera equipment is not always easy. I carry my gear in Lowepro camera backpacks. With a lighter complement of gear, use a waist pack or a big fanny pack. In either case, the objective is to keep your hands free when walking on uneven terrain.

Amazing photographs can be made with even the simplest of cameras. What camera equipment to use is beyond the scope of this guide, but here are a few things to consider. Use a camera with a manual exposure setting capability, and meter everything in a scene. Vistas pose the added challenge of a sky that is much brighter than the foreground, typically by several stops. A graduated neutral density filter is an essential tool; buy a good one. Because vistas have such a wide array of compositional possibilities, you'll end up using every lens you own, from an extreme wide-angle like a 17mm to a big telephoto like a 400mm, so bring them all. Put a polarizer on the camera and leave it on. Don't bother with a skylight or UV filter—they're worthless. Warming filters will add color to sunrise and sunset skies, but don't overdo it; stick to an 81A or 81B filter. Don't use warming filters during midday. Another handy filter to have is a 10CC magenta, which will enhance reds and pinks during twilight. Exposures longer than 1 second will be common at dusk and dawn, so a sturdy tripod that places the camera at eye level without extending the center post works best.

Photographing Vistas

Photography means to paint with light, and good lighting should drive when you shoot. You can take photographs at any hour of the day from any location, but here are some hints that will help you take more amazing shots:

- In the morning, start shooting before the sun comes up. In the evening, keep shooting after it goes down. Work the light until your camera can no longer provide exposure readings.

- Instead of shooting toward the sun, work with the light to your side or behind you. Sidelighting creates texture and shadows that separate hills and ridges, creating a three-dimensional effect. Side- and backlighting work especially well during fall.

- If there is thick cloud cover, be patient and wait for a "God beam"—a shaft of light through a hole in a cloud that spotlights the landscape. These are magical!

- Clearing and approaching storm fronts can create incredible cloud formations with magical colors like pink cotton candy. Keep abreast of changing weather patterns.

- Shoot every lens you own, starting with a wide-angle and finishing with a telephoto.

- Shoot until you run out film, digital storage space, or batteries.

A graduated neutral density filter is the most important tool to use when shooting vistas. This filter, which is gray on top and clear on the bottom, is used to even out or compensate exposures by darkening the sky so a scene can be recorded properly. They are either round, screw-type filters or square to allow for a changing horizon position. Get a square one with the appropriate filter mount for your camera. Cokin makes reasonably priced plastic sets. They also come in different intensities or shades of gray, listed as one-stop, two-stop, or three-stop filters, which darken the sky accordingly. I usually end up using a two-stop filter at dawn or dusk and a one-stop at midday. These filters also come in different edge types. A soft-edge filter has a smooth transition from clear to gray, whereas a hard-edge goes from clear to gray as a harsh line. I use both regularly.

To use a graduated filter, meter the foreground and record that value, then meter the sky near the horizon but not near the sun (the sun should never be part of a meter reading). Set your camera's exposure for the foreground reading, and then pick a graduated neutral density filter that will keep the sky at least one stop brighter than the foreground. In low or indirect light, such as from a twilight sky, use a gray card to meter the foreground. Bracket at least one stop on either side of what you expect, even when using digital cameras. Bracketing is cheap insurance.

When composing a photo, the biggest issue is where to put the horizon. It's usually not a good idea to place it in the middle of the frame. Generally, an image looks best when the horizon is placed in the top third of the frame. A basic premise of this idea is that you're photographing the landscape, not the sky, so don't include a lot of sky. But if the sky is where the magic is, then place the horizon in the bottom third of the frame. Whatever you do, just make sure the image looks balanced. It's also important to make sure the horizon is level.

I often see people come to a location, set up a tripod, shoot a couple frames, and then leave. They're really missing out, because the first view you see often isn't the best. Move left and right to change your perspective. Raise and lower your tripod. Get close to the edge, and then pull away. Put lots of foreground in the frame, and then none. Shoot every lens you own, beginning with a wide-angle and going longer and longer. Shoot twenty or thirty compositions from a location. Play with the scene until there is no room left on your memory card.

Most important, always remember to take joy in the moment. The pressure to capture the flaming light of dawn can be overwhelming. Take time to step back from the camera and soak in the sublime. Taking the road less traveled is about the experience, not the images. Focus on the experience, and magical images will surely follow. Enjoy!

| Hike 1 | **Rim Rock Overlook, Allegheny National Forest** |

Type: ledge	**Height:** 2,005 feet
Rating: 4	**Best time:** any time
GPS: 41° 50.573'N, 78° 56.786'W	**Difficulty:** easy; some rock hopping
Faces: 259°	**Distance:** .5 mile
Field of view: 196° to 322°	**Time:** 30 minutes
Relief: 45 feet	**Elevation change:** 70 feet
Elevation difference: 680 feet	**Best lenses:** 20mm to 75mm

Directions: From the intersection of US 6 and PA 59 in Rogertown (east of Warren), take PA 59 east for 12.4 miles, crossing the Cornplanter Bridge, and turn right onto Rim Rock Road (FR 454) near the top of a hill. Follow the paved road to a large dead-end parking area. GPS coordinates: 41° 50.653'N, 78° 56.780'W

This is the only decent series of Allegheny Reservoir views in the entire national forest. Another popular view to the west called Jakes Rock is completely overgrown, and until the Forest Service receives ample funding, it will remain so. Follow the paved path 100 yards down some stairs to two large, walled views. A narrow stairway between the views descends through a large cleft leading to the Rim Rock Trail. On the way down, make note of

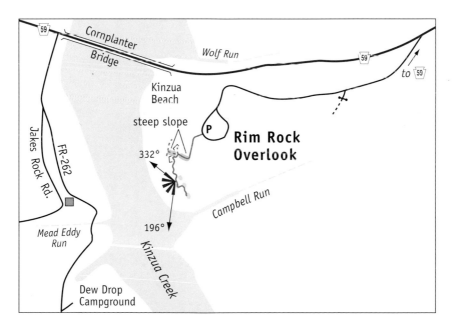

the thin laminae of sandstone and quartz pebbles that make up the massive conglomerate blocks on either side. Each sequence is a change in water flow rushing over a broad mountain outwash plain near the end of an ancient inland sea. The larger the quartz pebbles, the faster the flow. Like tree rings, these layers allow geologists to read the story left behind in the rocks. This story is nearly 300 million years old.

These two walled views are nice, but if you follow a prominent footpath to the left, you'll end up at two enormous boulders that provide much better exposure. Although the round-trip is .5 mile, once you get to the first walled viewpoint, the boulders are only about 120 yards farther. You'll quickly come to two large conglomerate blocks forming views separated by 30 yards. The first looks farther up the long axis of the reservoir, while the second looks more into a series of coves formed by Billies, Hodge, and North Runs. These are the best locations to shoot from.

Hike 2 Beartown Rocks, Clear Creek State Forest

Type: ridge	**Height:** 1,893 feet
Rating: 4+	**Best time:** any time is good, but near noon is best
GPS: 41° 18.208'N, 79° 3.599'W	**Difficulty:** easy
Faces: 320°	**Distance:** 200 yards
Field of view: 290° to 345°	**Time:** 10 minutes
Relief: 20 feet	**Elevation change:** 30 feet
Elevation difference: 469 feet	**Best lenses:** 50mm to 125mm

Directions: From the intersection of PA 36 and PA 949 in the village of Sigel, take PA 949 north for 4 miles, turning right onto Corbett Road. Follow Corbett, bearing left at a Y in .1 mile; then turn right in 2 miles at a sign for Beartown Rocks. Park in the dead-end parking area. GPS coordinates: 41° 18.175'N, 79° 3.631'W

An easy stroll and a short flight of stairs lead to the top of a massive boulder. With a wide exposure and decent relief, it provides an interesting northwesterly view along the Dry Run Creek shed looking toward the Clarion River. There was something about this view that impressed me a great deal. It's the only view in the heart of the Allegheny Plateau that has a northerly exposure, and it's best in early spring or during peak fall color. Near noon is best.

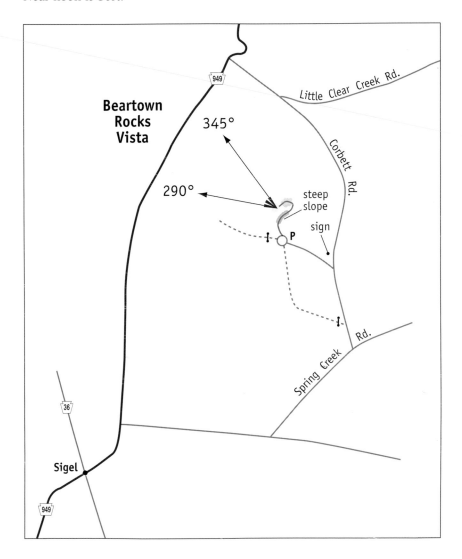

Hike 3 Pine Knob, Forbes State Forest

Type: ridge	Height: 2,107 feet
Rating: 3	Best times: midmorning through sunset
GPS: 39° 51.479′N, 79° 41.261′W	Difficulty: easy; woods road with few rocks and a short steep climb
Faces: 316°	Distance: .4 mile
Field of view: 262° to 10°	Time: 30 minutes
Relief: 10 feet	Elevation change: 100 feet
Elevation difference: 1,048 feet	Best lenses: 35mm to 75mm

Directions: From the US 40/US 119 interchange in Uniontown, take US 40 east for 6.5 miles, passing the entrance to the Lick Run Picnic Area. Turn right onto Sky Line Drive at the Laurel Caverns sign. In 2 miles, turn right onto an unnamed forest road. Follow this rough dirt road for 2.1 miles. At this point, the road may become a mud bog. If so, park here. If not, turn left and climb a steep road to where it's closed by boulders, a distance of 200 yards. GPS coordinates: 39° 51.373′N, 79° 41.258′W

This dirt road in an isolated section of Forbes State Forest looks worse than it is. Just take your time and avoid the deep mud holes where the road ends. From either parking place, walk up a steep hill for a short distance, following blue blazes to crest Pine Knob. The woods road trail leads directly to the viewpoint, which is a series of boulder ledges exposed on the northwest flank of Pine Knob. Small trees fill the foreground, but they're in good shape and don't spoil the view. How wide the view is in coming years will depend on maintenance. You can see the town of Hopwood close in and all of Uniontown farther away. The most natural view is to the west, where US 119 dissolves into green farm fields.

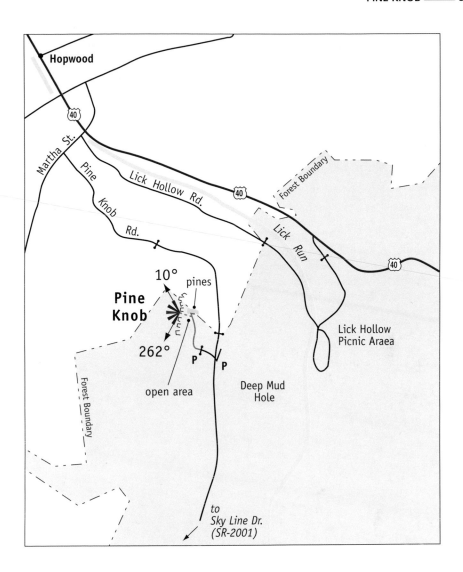

Hopwood

Martha St.

40

Pine

Knob

Rd.

Lick Hollow Rd.

40

Forest Boundary

Lick Run

40

10°

pines

**Pine
Knob**

262°

P

P

open area

Forest Boundary

Deep Mud
Hole

Lick Hollow
Picnic Araea

*to
Sky Line Dr.
(SR-2001)*

Hike 4 Mount Davis High Point Tower, Forbes State Forest

Type: ridge	**Elevation difference:** 557 feet
Rating: 4	**Height:** 3,213 feet
GPS: 39° 47.155'N, 79° 10.602'W	**Best time:** any time
Faces: panorama	**Trail:** none
Field of view: panorama	**Elevation change:** 50-foot tower climb
Relief: 50 feet	**Best lenses:** 35mm to 100mm

Directions: From Somerset, take US 219 south for 19 miles to Meyersdale, and exit onto Mason Dixon Highway north. In Meyersdale, it becomes Beachly Street. Bear left onto Grant; then turn left onto Broadway Street. In .3 mile, Broadway crosses a railroad. Turn right onto Mount Davis Road (SR 2004), which has numerous turns and intersections but always maintains both name and route number. In 9.8 miles, turn left onto South Vought Rock Road to enter the Mount Davis Natural Area, and in .7 mile, turn left again into the parking area. GPS coordinates: 39° 47.178'N, 79° 10.610'W

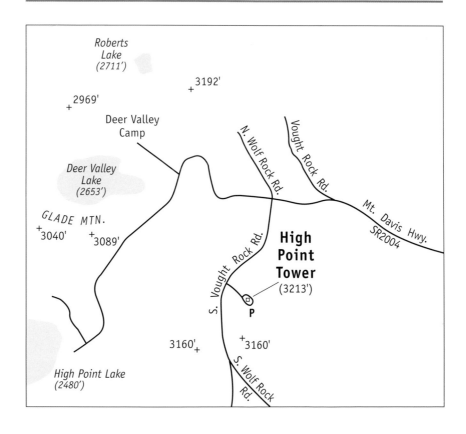

Roberts Lake (2711')

3192'

2969'

Deer Valley Camp

Deer Valley Lake (2653')

N. Wolf Rock Rd.

Vought Rock Rd.

Mt. Davis Hwy. SR2004

GLADE MTN.
3040'   3089'

High Point Tower
(3213')

S. Vought Rock Rd.

P

3160'   3160'

High Point Lake (2480')

S. Wolf Rock Rd.

One would expect the state's highest point to stand hundreds or thousands of feet above the surrounding terrain and provide an incredible view. It doesn't. High Point is merely the highest knob among a great many knobs studding the broad, flat ridge of Negro Mountain. The five nearest knobs, which are within a mile, stand not more than 100 feet shorter. Near the tower is the USGS high-point marker, a bronze disk cemented to a boulder among the trees. Look around and note how all the surrounding trees are stunted and gnarly from the constant wind and some of the worst weather in the state.

What it lacks in majesty, Mount Davis makes up for in how far you can see. On the clearest days, the view can be up to 60 miles. The tower has an interesting set of plaques identifying various terrain features. With a rather small deck, the tower has room for only six people—that is, if you don't mind getting close—and the narrow stairwell requires patience. Nearby High Point Lake is not the highest in the state. That honor goes to Roberts Lake, at 2,711 feet elevation.

For me, the best thing about Mount Davis is the quiet. When the wind stops blowing and no other people are around, the gnarly forest sucks all sound out of the air, and the quiet is almost painful. It's really kind of weird.

Shanksville and the Flight 93 Memorial are only 21 miles away in a straight line to the northeast. Go visit, and take along some tissues—you'll need them. When I worked this area on Memorial Day weekend, my wife and I made it a point to spend time there. It was a profound moment, to say the least.

Hike 5 Laurel Hill, Laurel Ridge State Park

Type: ledge	**Height:** 2,919 feet
Rating: 4	**Best times:** late morning through sunset
GPS: 39° 58.960′N, 79° 21.127′W	**Difficulty:** easy
Faces: 274°	**Distance:** .8 mile
Field of view: 238° to 310°	**Time:** 45 minutes
Relief: 20 feet	**Elevation change:** 20 feet
Elevation difference: 1,117 feet	**Best lenses:** 20mm to 200mm

Directions: The last mile of this drive requires high clearance. From Somerset, take PA 281 south for 8.1 miles, and pick up PA 653 south in New Centerville. Take PA 653 north/west for 8.2 miles, and turn right onto King Mountain Road. Follow King Mountain for 2.3 miles, passing a golf course at .5 mile, where King Mountain changes names to become Earl Ansell Road. At a confusing road junction with few road signs, to your left is Robin Lane and ahead is the junction of Cardinal and Sparrow Lanes. Off to the left, sort of catty-corner, is Earl Ansell Road (T 316), a rough road looking like a driveway that climbs the flank of a small hill. Bear left around a cabin to follow this drivable trail uphill. In .5 mile, the road turns and forms a T intersection with John Henry Road (there are no signs). Turn right and follow this narrow rocky road .1 mile to where it makes a hard left. On the right is large, open field. Find a wide spot on the right and park. GPS coordinates: 39° 59.165′N, 79° 20.836′W

Sky Glow on Rocks. Heavy haze and high humidity can make shooting sunset impossible, but the sky will glow warmly after the sun goes down. That's when you shoot the effect of indirect skylight on the foreground. *Tachihara 4x5 field camera, 75mm Rodenstock Grandagon f/6.8, 2-stop graduate, 10CC magenta, 4x5 Ready Load holder, Kodak E100VS, f/32 @ 5 sec.*

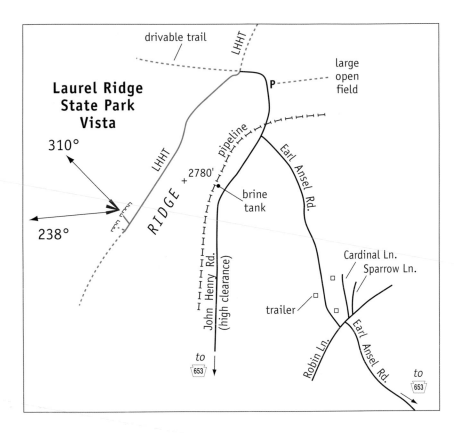

Laurel Ridge
State Park
Vista

310°

238°

drivable trail

LHHT

large
open
field

P

RIDGE

LHHT

pipeline

× 2780'

brine
tank

Earl Ansel Rd.

John Henry Rd.
(high clearance)

Cardinal Ln.
Sparrow Ln.

trailer

Earl Ansel Rd.

Robin Ln.

to
653

to
653

Finding the parking area is a lot more difficult than this short, level hike. From the parking area, with the open field to your back, walk a few yards down the road to where a boot path crosses. This is the Laurel Highlands Trail, which runs for more than 40 miles from Ohiopyle State Park to near Johnstown. Turn left (south) and follow this delightful path for .4 mile to two large rock outcroppings on the right. This is the view. The first rock ledge you come to is the better of the two, photographically speaking. It has a wide eroded fissure that makes a nice leading line. What I love about this location is how the ledges are eroded into natural lounge chairs where you can while away hours in sandstone comfort.

Although the elevation difference is listed as over 1,000 feet, it doesn't look like it. The small drainage nearest you is the middle fork of Buck Run, which provides the opening for the view. Because the middle fork falls away gently, the view doesn't seem as high as what a topo map shows. Although the Laurel Highlands Trail guide notes dozens of viewpoints, this is the only one that isn't partially or totally overgrown.

Hike 6 Wolf Rocks, Linn Run State Park

Type: ledge	**Height:** 2,667 feet
Rating: 3+	**Best times:** late morning through sunset
GPS: 40° 8.236'N, 79° 11.883'W	**Difficulty:** easy
Faces: 237°	**Distance:** 4.2 miles
Field of view: 168° to 306°	**Time:** 2 hours
Relief: 30 feet	**Elevation change:** 125 feet
Elevation difference: 372 feet	**Best lenses:** 20mm to 200mm

Directions: From the intersection of PA 381 and US 30 east of Ligonier, take PA 381 south for 1.4 miles. Turn left onto Linn Run Road and follow for 7.2 miles, passing through the park, and turn left onto Laurel Summit Road. In .6 mile, pull into a large picnic area on the left and park in the large lot beyond the bathrooms. GPS coordinates: 40° 7.101'N, 79° 10.547'W

Exit the parking area at the large Wolf Rocks Trail sign, and follow the wide, sometimes rocky, and thoroughly enjoyable trail. At .53 mile, you come to a junction with Spruce Flats and Wolf Rocks Loop Trails. Stay on the red-blazed Wolf Rocks Trail. Rocks begin to appear, becoming progressively larger and jutting through the soil at 1.3 miles. When the Wolf Rocks Loop Trail rejoins at 1.66 miles, continue straight ahead on the red-blazed Wolf Rocks Trail. Just beyond, you reach an intersection with the Bobcat

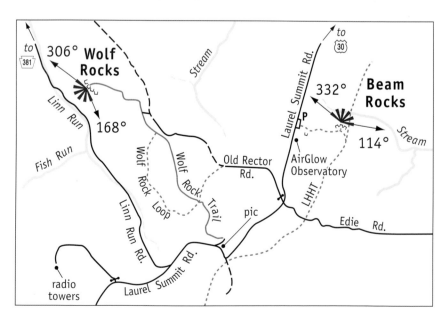

Trail, which is marked by a sign. Stick with the Wolf Rocks Trail, arriving at the majestic view at 2.1 miles.

Unseen but readily heard is Linn Run, which can be overwhelmed by traffic noise. The view is mostly of Bald Knob Ridge opposite, which has radio towers on it at 197°. Providing the most visual interest is a triple divide valley of Spruce, Linn, and Fish Runs on the left. Wolf Rocks is best in fall, and since the level trail can be skied or snowshoed, it also makes a great winter location.

Hike 7 Beam Rocks, Linn Run State Park

Type: ledge	**Height:** 2,667 feet
Rating: 3	**Best times:** late morning through sunset
GPS: 40° 7.952'N, 79° 9.416'W	**Difficulty:** easy
Faces: 42°	**Distance:** .9 mile
Field of view: 332° to 114°	**Time:** 30 minutes
Relief: 45 feet	**Elevation change:** 150 feet
Elevation difference: 372 feet	**Best lenses:** 20mm to 300mm

Directions: From the intersection of PA 381 and US 30 east of Ligonier, take PA 381 south for 1.4 miles. Turn left onto Linn Run Road and follow for 7.2 miles, passing through the park, and turn left onto Laurel Summit Road. In .6 mile, just beyond the large Laurel Summit Picnic Area, bear left onto Laurel Ridge Road. In 1.4 miles, park on the right at the Beam Rocks trailhead. GPS coordinates: 40° 7.970'N, 79° 9.832'W

This short trail brings you to a series of exposed boulders and ledges that look northeast along the shallow flank of Laurel Ridge (see map on p. 10). Simply walk down the wide, improved blue blazed trail to the viewpoint. The best view is looking along the view's extreme right along an axis of 90° or 100°. This direction looks out on farm fields and the village of Gray sitting 3.5 miles away. Boulders that make up the view have small potholes, which are formed when rain reacts with the calcium in the stone to form carbonic acid. This weak acid slowly eats the stone to form the pockmarked surface. Come here after a rain so that full potholes add interest to the foreground. If that's not possible, pack extra water and fill a few of them to achieve this effect. It's also a good idea to bring a whisk broom, as there is a great deal of broken glass around.

Hike 8   Blankley Road, Buchanan State Forest

Rainsburg

Type: ridge	**Field of view:** 320° to 360°
Rating: 3	**Relief:** 10 feet
GPS: 39° 52.037'N, 77° 31.400'W	**Elevation Difference:** 944 feet
Faces: 345°	**Height:** 2,298 feet

Warrior Ridge

Type: ridge	**Field of view:** 110° to 190°
Rating: 4	**Relief:** 10 feet
GPS: 39° 52.198'N, 78° 30.904'W	**Elevation Difference:** 890 feet
Faces: 150°	**Height:** 2,163 feet
Best times: morning through afternoon	**Elevation change:** none
Trail: none	**Best lenses:** 35mm to 125mm

Directions: From Bedford, take US 30 east for 1.7 miles to PA 326 south. Follow PA 326 for 11.3 miles, going through the town of Rainsburg. Where PA 326 passes through a mountain gap, turn right onto gravel Blankley Road. Warrior Ridge is .5 mile on the left, and Rainsburg is 1 mile on the right.

In spring and summer Warrior Ridge Vista renders as an uninteresting mass of green. In fall, however, the riot of color combined with the overlapping hills creates a great deal of visual interest. *Canon EOS Digital Rebel, Tamron 28–200, polarizer, 1 stop graduate, ISO100 setting, f16 @ 1/8 sec.*

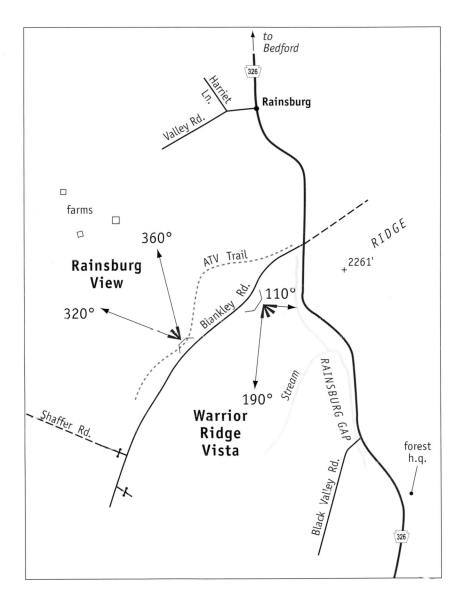

to
Bedford

326

Rainsburg

Harriet Ln.

Valley Rd.

farms

360°

Rainsburg
View

ATV Trail

RIDGE

+2261'

320°

Blankley Rd.

110°

190°

Stream

RAINSBURG GAP

Warrior
Ridge
Vista

Shaffer Rd.

forest
h.q.

Black Valley Rd.

326

Neither view is more than several paces walking. Warrior Ridge looks southeasterly toward the ridge bearing its name and the narrow valley of Sweet Root Creek. But the better view is Rainsburg, which looks out on a bowl-shaped cove. Setting up on the left provides an excellent view of three or four farms below. The nearest farm has a barn with a white roof, so low light will work best here. This view is a first-rate spot in fall, with the tree-lined ridges surrounding the cove valley offsetting the farm fields nicely.

Hike 9 Tower Road, Tuscarora Trail, Buchanan State Forest

Type: ledge	Height: 2,368 feet
Rating: 5+	Best times: sunrise through midmorning
GPS: 39° 57.017'N, 77° 56.203'W	Difficulty: easy to moderate, depending on whether road is open
Faces: 90°	Distance: 100 feet when Tower Road is open; 1.8 miles if road is closed by snow
Field of view: 25° to 160°	Time: 1 hour when road is closed
Relief: 25 feet	Elevation change: 260 feet for the road hike
Elevation difference: 1,790 feet	Best lenses: 30mm to 200mm

Directions: From McConnellsburg, take US 30 east for 3.6 miles to where it crests Tuscarora Mountain. As you ascend, look for two wooden platforms on the exposed ridge crest. When the blue highway sign announcing the summit comes into view, turn left onto Augwhick Road (SR 1005). In .9 mile, bear right onto Tower Road, and follow it to where it ends in a large parking loop. If the road is closed by snow, park where it diverges from Augwhick Road.

I had been frustrated by the lack of good views in Tuscarora State Forest, but then a ranger from nearby Cowans Gap State Park told me he liked to drive up to the end of Tower Road because it has a "pretty good view." Pretty good is a severe understatement—the view is incredible!

If the road is open, make the short walk toward a gap in the trees, and step down onto a rocky outcrop. If the road is closed by snow, snowshoe 1.8 miles up the road; or for some fun, head several dozen yards east along the Lincoln Trail, and then turn left and follow the blue-blazed Tuscarora Trail for 1.8 miles to the view.

The ledge you're on is divided by a gap, creating two distinct shooting perches. The upper provides the best view to the southeast, while the lower avoids a scraggly pine tree to open a better northeast view. Unfortunately, the stone outcrops have been painted gray to cover graffiti, so you won't be able shoot rock patterns as foregrounds. The view right is a long-lens shot, while the view left is a normal to wide shot.

Looking down on Path Valley, you can see where the valley narrows south of Richmond Furnace on your right and broadens toward the northeast as the west branch of Conococheague Creek meanders down from Fannettsburg, which is the town to the left in the far distance. It's impossible to shoot at twilight from here without valley fog. The entire valley is filled with lights, and brightly lit Carlisle seems to hover in midair to the east.

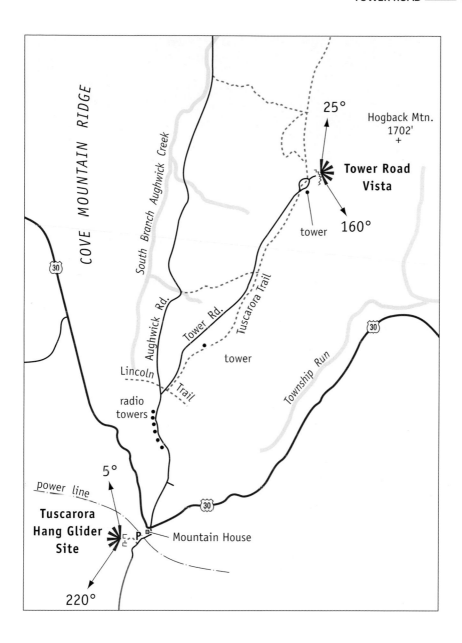

Hike 10 Tuscarora Summit Hang Glider Launch Site, Franklin County

Type: ridge	**Height:** 2,152 feet
Rating: 4	**Best times:** early afternoon through sunset
GPS: 39° 54.859′N, 77° 57.534′W	**Difficulty:** easy
Faces: 285°	**Distance:** 100 feet
Field of view: 220° to 5°	**Time:** a few minutes
Relief: 10 feet	**Elevation change:** 30 feet
Elevation difference: 1,136 feet	**Best lenses:** 20mm to 400mm

Directions: From McConnellsburg, take US 30 east for 3.6 miles to where it crests Tuscarora Mountain. As you ascend, look for two wooden platforms on the exposed ridge crest. When the blue highway sign announcing the summit comes into view, turn right into the Mountain House Restaurant parking area. Pass by the building on your right by following a dirt lane. Cross a power line and look for a gravel parking area on the right in about 100 yards. Two large wooden launch platforms will be in view atop the ridge.

Walk up the wide, grassy area past the benches, and set up between the two platforms, closer to the left one than the right. Do not attempt to set up equipment *on* the platforms, as they are pitched rather steeply and there's a 10-foot drop off the end onto sandstone boulders.

Looking down on McConnellsburg from so high up provides a pleasing view of cloud shadows as they move across Cove Valley. The ever-present wind is why the launch platforms are here, so even though the wind might be calm in the valley, be prepared for stiff breezes buffeting your equipment here on the ridge. Besides being a mountain view, it's also a good place to watch the fall hawk migration.

Restricting a wide-angle shot of McConnellsburg is the JLG Power Lift factory at 304° only 1.6 miles away, with a storage yard full of bright orange equipment. You'll have to work compositions and lighting very carefully to keep the pale roof and white concrete parking area out of frame. The view with the least problems is to the left, looking out over Cove Valley toward Little Scrub Ridge. The large mountain in the far distance is Sideling Hill, home of two more launch sites.

Magic Carpet Ride. Shooting at Tower Road, I turned and caught a glimpse of a hang glider to my south. I broke down my gear and drove as fast as safety would allow to get to this spot. When I arrived, this was the last person in the air. Seeing my long lens, she asked me where I wanted her. I asked if she could keep north of the sun for few minutes. "Sure, no problem!" she yelled down. I changed lenses, and for the next ten minutes, she waved back and forth over the valley in front me. With the wind dying, she drifted south and landed. What a moment! *Canon EOS Digital Rebel, Tokina 20–35, polarizer, ISO100 setting, f/8 @ 1/40 sec.*

Hike 11 Bark Road, Buchanan State Forest

Type: ridge	**Height:** 2,158 feet
Rating: 5	**Best times:** sunrise through late morning
GPS: 40° 0.125'N, 78° 7.828'W	**Difficulty:** easy
Faces: 120°	**Distance:** 100 feet
Field of view: 20° to 195°	**Time:** a few minutes
Relief: 20 feet	**Elevation change:** none
Elevation difference: 1,177 feet	**Best lenses:** 17mm to 200mm

Directions: From Breezewood, take US 30 east for 5 miles from the I-70 interchange. Just as you pass PA 915 on your left, turn right into a picnic area. Then follow Bark Road around to the east flank of Sideling Hill, arriving at the view in 1.8 miles. Park adjacent to the boulders on the right.

The state forest picnic area on US 30 is where everybody stops to admire the view because they don't know what's around the bend of Bark Road—another picnic area with an astonishing view. Just walk past the boulders for 100 feet at most to arrive at a rocky outcrop nearly 30 yards wide. Find a comfortable spot to spread out your favorite picnic blanket. It's a bucolic scene marred only by a large chicken house with a silver roof at 124° about a mile off. It shouldn't be a problem by dawn's early light.

While I sat jotting notes on a beautiful April afternoon, a kettle of vultures boiled up through the warming air, making lazy circles no more than 100 yards away. Drifting slowly closer, they eventually arrived at eye level and were so close I could hear the wind moving through their wingtip feathers. As the vultures disappeared overhead, I noticed a couple of turkey hens scratching the ground near my truck. Enough people picnic here that these normally wary birds didn't mind my moving around to get a better look at them. Eventually they wandered across the road into the woods.

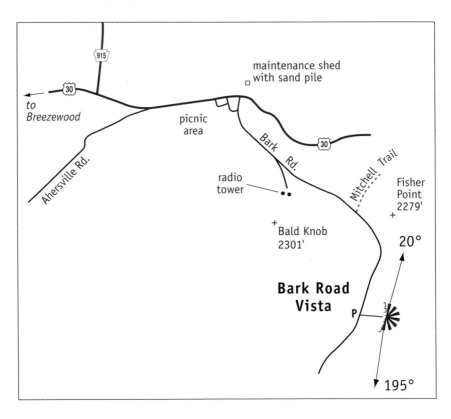

World on Fire. "Red sky in morning, sailor's warning" is very true. Less than thirty minutes after this shot, it began to rain and flurry. The foreground trees glowed for about five minutes before their color slowly bled away. *Canon EOS Rebel Xs, Tokina 20–35, 2-stop graduate, 81A warming filter, Kodak E100VS, f/27 @ 8 sec.*

Hike 12 Summit Road Hang Glider Launch Site, Buchanan State Forest

Type: ridge	**Elevation difference:** 881 feet
Rating: 5+	**Height:** 1,876 feet
GPS: 40° 5.355'N, 78° 5.509'W	**Best times:** sunrise through late morning
Faces: 117°	**Trail:** none
Field of view: 50° to 160°	**Elevation change:** none
Relief: 10 feet	**Best lenses:** 17mm to 400mm

Directions: From Breezewood, take US 30 east for 4.5 miles from the I-70 interchange, and turn left onto PA 915 north. Take PA 915 north for 2.4 miles, turning right onto Summit Road after you pass over the turnpike. You will arrive at the view in 2.3 miles. If the road is closed by snow, you can hike up the Woodcock Trail from Enid Road (T 445) 1 mile east of PA 915 and the village of Enid.

ooking out from Sideling Hill's narrow crest into Shore Valley reminds me of the old joke about sky diving: "It's not the fall that'll kill you, but the sudden stop at the end." Hang gliders, like their parachuting cousins, accept a certain amount of risk for the love of their sport. Fortunately, you don't have to in order to appreciate this incredible view. The view has few foreground issues except for some fluttering pieces of red vinyl used by pilots to gauge wind speed. During midday, a polarizer won't have much effect on the sky, but it will knock down the sheen of foreground brush.

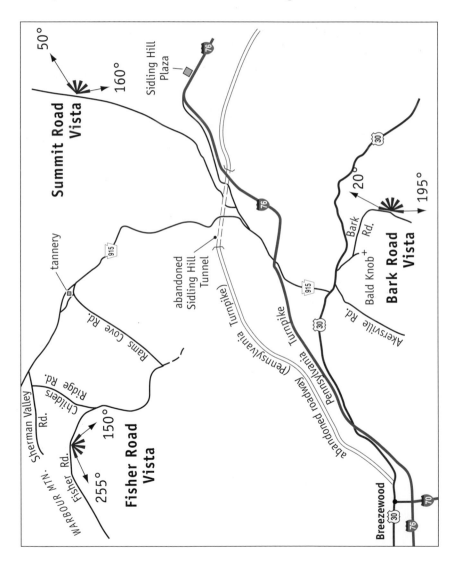

Fall Peak. Midday shooting is never a problem when the air is clear. In this case, a nice cloud deck enhances the scene. *Canon EOS Digital Rebel, Tokina 20–35, polarizer, 1-stop graduate, ISO100 setting, f/8 @ 1/60 sec.*

Hike 13 Fisher Road Hang Glider Launch Site, Buchanan State Forest

Type: ridge	**Elevation difference:** 805 feet
Rating: 5+	**Height:** 2,226 feet
GPS: 40° 5.413'N, 78° 13.027'W	**Best times:** good any time, but best from sunrise through late morning
Faces: 200°	**Trail:** none
Field of view: 150° to 255°	**Elevation change:** none
Relief: 10 feet	**Best lenses:** 17mm to 200mm

Directions: From Breezewood, take US 30 east for 4.5 miles from the I-70 interchange, and turn left onto PA 915 north. Take PA 915 north for 8.2 miles, turning left onto Sherman Valley Road (SR 1020). In .3 mile, make another left onto Childers Ridge Road. Follow Childers to a Y intersection with Fisher Road in 1.3 miles, and make a hard right onto Fisher Road. In .8 mile, look for a dirt lane that climbs steeply on the left. Turn left and park in an open area facing the view. Be sure to set your parking brake.

This is an incredible view! Located in the northernmost curve of Harbor Mountain, where it joins Sideling Hill, the viewpoint looks southwest over a wide valley created by a long series of looping meanders of the Raystown Branch of the Juniata River. Raystown Lake is behind you. Breezewood is to the left, and fortunately it's completely hidden by Sideling Hill. Also to the left, Bedford is hidden by intervening ridges. The stiff prevailing wind is why hang gliders come here. During fall color, this is a tremendous place in early-morning or late-afternoon light.

Hike 14 Priceless Point, Standing Stone Trail, State Game Lands 81

Monument Rock

Type: cobble	**Field of view:** 230° to 315°
Rating: 5+	**Relief:** 15 feet
GPS: 40° 5.795′N, 77° 56.668′W	**Elevation difference:** 597 feet
Faces: 270°	**Height:** 1,341 feet

Priceless Ledge

Type: ledge	**Field of view:** 90° to 186°
Rating: 5	**Relief:** 25 feet
GPS: 40° 5.314′N, 77° 56.230′W	**Elevation difference:** 979 feet
Faces: 140°	**Height:** 1,853 feet

Priceless Point

Type: cobble	**Field of view:** 20° to 150
Rating: 5+	**Relief:** 15 feet
GPS: 40° 5.343′N, 77° 56.165′W	**Elevation difference:** 957 feet
Faces: 85°	**Height:** 1,795 feet
Best times: sunrise through sunset	**Time:** 3 hours, 15 minutes
Difficulty: moderate	**Elevation change:** 1,425 feet
Distance: 5.2 miles	**Best lenses:** 17mm to 300mm

Directions: Exit the PA Turnpike (I-76) at exit 180, and turn right onto US 522 east. Follow for .8 mile into Fort Littleton, and turn left onto Sinoquipe Road (SR 1011) north. After 2.6 miles, look for blue blazes on telephone poles on the left. Park on the west side of the road opposite house number 2702. GPS coordinates: 40° 5.905′N, 77° 57.367′W

These three amazing views along the Standing Stone Trail are fairly easy to get to and beg to be shot in every kind of light. The last 100 yards from Priceless Ledge to Priceless Point are a bit challenging, but the hike is worth the effort for perhaps one of the best mountain views Penn's Woods has to offer.

Walk south past the driveway opposite where you parked for 20 or 30 yards, and look for a brown sign tucked in the trees on the left indicating the Standing Stone Trail and Ramsey Path. Turn left and climb the bank. You're on private land—please act accordingly. The Ramsey Path is blazed blue. The red paint blobs you see are survey marks, so ignore these and follow the blue blazes.

In about 200 yards, you come to a double blaze indicating a right turn. Directly ahead is a No Trespassing sign. Shortly after you cross the old McKelvey Railroad grade at .1 mile, turn right to join a woods road. Look behind you here and make note of a No Trespassing sign that will mark the return route. Cross into state game lands at .45 mile, marked by an orange placard on the left that has a blue blaze and private land notice on the back. Shortly after the woods road, the trail makes a sweeping right to come parallel to a drainage on the left. At the head of this drainage, the trail sweeps left.

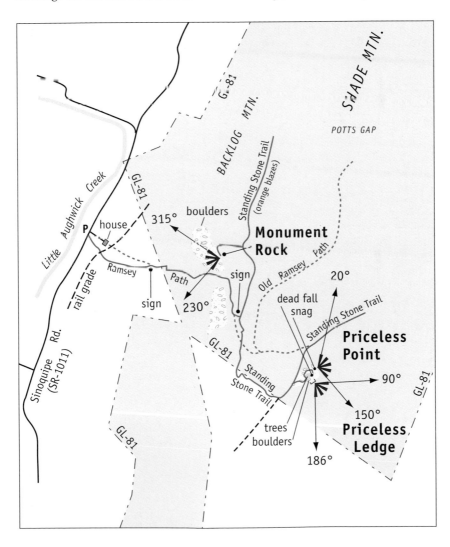

Near .7 mile, the base of a rock fall or cobble can be seen through the trees on the left. At the base of this expanse of rock, turn right as indicated by a double blaze. Just beyond, look high above on the left for sedimentary rocks turned nearly vertical. You're passing through a fault line created by the collision of Blacklog and Shade Mountains, the force of which is evident on both sides of the trail.

After passing through the fault line, the trail follows a gap in the ridge by turning right at .86 mile. As you move along, the sides of the gap begin to close in, and at 1 mile, you cross a seep or damp area. Shortly after, the trail switchbacks left up a slope to bring you to the orange-blazed Standing Stone Trail at 1.14 miles. The trail is noted by an orange game-lands placard with a blue blaze on the post, denoting your return route using the Ramsey Path.

From this point, a left turn will take you to Monument Rock and a right to Priceless Point. Turn left. The trail is fairly level and well blazed, so don't be afraid to set a brisk pace. The trail jogs from the ridge's right side to the left at 1.3 miles. At 1.5 miles, you'll see another game-lands placard with a marker for the vista. Here the orange-blazed Standing Stone Trail turns right to climb, but instead go straight along the blue-blazed vista trail, which descends through open woods. As the trees begin to open ahead, make a sharp left at 1.64 miles at the head of a cobble. A few yards farther along, you arrive at a splendid west-facing view.

Monument Rock is not the cobble, but a solitary vertical stone pillar to your left that stands watch over a handsome valley filled with rolling hills and ridges. While I was jotting notes on a hot afternoon, two vultures came into view well below me. When they found the thermal created by the 2-acre cobble, they began a series of lazy circles, coming ever closer to pick up a freshening breeze off the ridgetop. Either checking me for signs of life or merely curious, they turned their heads to observe me during each repetition. Moments like this are why it's good to sit quietly and allow the sublime to come your way.

Return to the blue-blazed vista trail and make the quick climb back to the Standing Stone Trail, arriving at the intersection at 1.84 miles. Continue ahead along the orange-blazed trail (do not turn left to go uphill), and return to the head of the Ramsey Path at 2.28 miles. Follow the Standing Stone Trail and in 100 feet make a hard right where it turns to follow a woods road and begins to climb. For the next 100-plus yards, there are no blazes, so if you're hiking in the dark for sunrise, you'll know you're in the right place if you're on a climbing woods road. Be careful, however, because at 2.56 miles, the trail makes a surprising left turn at a private land marker. Although well marked by double orange blazes on the left and several white paint blobs on surrounding trees, it's the kind of thing you can miss when hustling to beat the light. The trail then bears right and heads straight uphill along the game-lands boundary. At 2.76 miles, turn left onto the woods road again, which is also marked by blazes and white paint blobs. Continue climbing and top out in 70 yards.

Monument Rock. Rapidly changing light and a stiff breeze made for challenging work. I had to wait ten minutes for light to hit the trees below the cobble. You have to be patient. Knowing when not to shoot is as important as knowing how. *Tachihara 4x5 field camera, 150mm Schneider Symmar f/5.6, polarizer, 2-stop graduate, 6x7 roll film back, Kodak E100VS, f/22 @ ¹/2 sec.*

As you continue on in the early-morning hours, you'll begin to notice daylight through the trees on the right. That's where you're headed. At 3 miles, turn right onto an unsigned blue-blazed trail. This side trail to Priceless Point is well blazed and climbs up through a small cobble, then turns left to follow the ridge crest. You'll have to pick your way around and under tree limbs to get to Priceless Ledge, which is an east-facing rock ledge located at 3.1 miles.

Looking out upon a wide valley with Tuscarora Mountain beyond, you can see where the turnpike makes a long easterly turn to line up with Tuscarora Tunnel. To the right is the nose of Cove Mountain where it folds over on itself to form Scrub Ridge at Sidneys Knob. Near the right limit of the view is a notch in the nearest tall ridge. This gap is where Nine Mile Run empties the north end of the Cove, which is a hanging valley formed by the folded ridge. It's a fine view, but better is yet to come if you don't mind some boulder hopping.

Continue along the blue-blazed trail, keeping the drop-off to your right. In a dozen yards, a double blaze on a rock indicates a left turn downslope. Before continuing, it's important to make note of what's below. Directly ahead are dense trees with a large, open cobble below that faces northeast. That cobble is Priceless Point. The problem is that you can't just take a direct line to get there. The indicated left turn is the last blaze, which is no real help. Turn left and work downslope a few yards to where you can see the boulder field below, and then stop to assess your ability, because from here the route to Priceless Point passes through a steep boulder fall with large, unsecured rocks that create potentially hazardous footing.

Priceless Point. Morning light was changing rapidly and the tree glow was fading when I realized I had only three sheets of 4x5 film left. Oops! *Tachihara 4x5 field camera, 75mm Rodenstock Grandagon f/6.8, 2-stop graduate, 81A warming filter, 4x5 Ready Load holder, Kodak E100VS, f/32 @ 8 sec.*

If you decide to continue, descend below the treeline onto the crunchy rock-tripe-encrusted boulders. Rock tripe is in the lichen family, and according to Bill Casselman's book *Canadian Food Words,* the name derives from the French *tripe de roché* meaning "rock guts." Believe it or not, it's edible as a "survival food." Apparently Washington's troops were forced to eat rock tripe at Valley Forge, which just proves that the Continentals were indeed a tough bunch of soldiers.

Turn right and follow a line around the cobble's head, keeping far enough below the treeline that you're using rocks with more exposed surface than brown tripe cover. Alternate watching where your feet are stepping and the boulders ahead. In dry conditions, rock tripe crumbles underfoot like peanut shells. If you get here for sunrise, however, the tripe will have absorbed enough dew to become slick like damp leather, making for difficult footing.

As you come around to the cobble's north side, the amount of tripe begins to decrease, until on the sunlit side it's all but gone. Once you've reached the northeast exposure, work back upslope, passing over a large deadfall and taking a position such that a tall standing dead tree is below and to your left. Facing east, you can see the turnpike, which you can easily eliminate from compositions. A pine with a dead top near the cobble's base is not an issue in morning light; in fact, as a natural part of the scene, it will hold up in any shot when lit by the warm light of sunrise.

The view here is fantastic and will easily make anybody's top-five list of mountain views. A number of low hills keep the roads in the valley from being visible, even US 522, which sweeps in fairly close, and the power-line cuts over Tuscarora Mountain aren't close enough to affect your images. There are photographic options galore here, so spend as much time as you can spare. I suggest starting with a wide-angle to fill the foreground with the cobble, and then working longer to pick out farms in the valley or overlapping shadows in Locke Valley to the left north of Potts Gap.

Reverse your route to work back up to the blue blazes, and then return to the orange-blazed Standing Stone Trail at 3.3 miles. Heading back downhill, continue to reverse your route, arriving at the blue-blazed Ramsey Path at 4 miles. At 5.14 miles, turn left to descend to the parking area. Don't forget the private land marker where the Ramsey Path turns to avoid the house whose driveway you parked near. Having hiked hundreds of miles working on this project, I can honestly say this has become one of my favorite trails. I certainly hope you enjoy it as much as I have.

Hike 15 The Throne Room, Standing Stone Trail, Rothrock State Forest

Hall of the Mountain King

Type: cobble	Field of view: 226° to 330° and 72° to 154°
Rating: 4	Relief: 5 feet
GPS: 40° 18.780'N, 77° 57.737'W	Elevation difference: 1,380 feet
Faces: 278° and 113°	Height: 2,206 feet

King's Chambers

Type: ledge	Field of view: 77° to 175°
Rating: 5	Relief: 25 feet
GPS: 40° 18.809'N, 77° 57.709'W	Elevation difference: 1,438 feet
Faces: 126°	Height: 2,265 feet

The Throne Room

Type: cobble	Field of view: 310° to 120°
Rating: 5+	Relief: 10 feet
GPS: 40° 18.963'N, 77° 57.699'W	Elevation difference: 1,321 feet
Faces: 35°	Height: 2,147 feet

Butler Knob

Type: cobble	Field of view: 130° to 245°
Rating: 5	Relief: 15 feet
GPS: 40° 17.523'N, 77° 58.012'W	Elevation difference: 1,706 feet
Faces: 190°	Height: 2,306 feet

Best times: sunrise through sunset	**Distance:** Butler Knob 100 yards
Distance: The Throne Room 3.8 miles	**Time:** 20 minutes
Time: 2 hours, 45 minutes	**Elevation change:** The Throne Room 320 feet, Butler Knob none
Difficulty: easy	**Difficulty:** easy
Best lenses: 17mm to 200mm	

Directions: To get to the Standing Stone Trailhead for The Throne Room, from the intersection of US 22 and US 522 in Mount Union, take US 22 west for about .4 mile to the Jefferson Street bridge/PA 747, and turn left to cross the bridge. You are now on Jefferson Street. Follow the signs for PA 747 south by turning left onto East Shirley, then in one block turning right onto North Division. Take PA 747 south out of town for 9.6 miles, and turn right onto White Road (T 367). Marking the turn, look for Gabert Road (T 368) on the left. Follow White Road for 100 yards, and turn right onto the unmarked gravel Park Road, which looks like a driveway passing between two houses. Follow the sometimes rough dirt and gravel road for 4.8 miles to a three-car-wide parking area on the left, with a sign for Ravens View. (Park Road passes through State Game Lands 99 and is not well maintained, but it is accessible by passenger car if you take your time.) If you dead-end at an antenna complex, you went about .25 mile too far. GPS coordinates: 40° 17.808'N, 77° 57.961'W

  To get to Butler Knob, continue to the antenna array and park near the old fire tower, being careful to avoid all the broken glass. A stone cabin with the number 132 painted in white on the roof should be on your left. The trail is a wide, grassy road to the right, heading for a gap in the trees. GPS coordinates: 40° 17.586'N, 77° 58.014'W

Hall of the Mountain King, the King's Chambers, and the Throne Room

Getting to the parking area doesn't require an SUV, it only seems that way.

  Walk past the sign for Ravens View, and follow the orange-blazed Standing Stone Trail into the woods. In a dozen yards, you come to the yellow gate of a deer exclosure. Lift the gate and pass through the fence. As you make your way along, large gaps to the right provide an appetizer of what's to come. The trail is almost overgrown in places, so wear long pants even when it's hot. At .28 mile, you exit the deer exclosure and then quickly enter another, which you'll exit at .51 mile.

  The trail rises and falls slightly as it meanders along. At a little under 1 mile, openings begin to appear on the left and right. By now you've passed by Ravens View, which is really not worth the time. At 1 mile, you enter private land marked by white paint blobs. Gradually the trail becomes more rocky and troublesome, and while you're intently looking down to watch your footing, you enter the Hall of the Mountain King at 1.2 miles.

  This huge ridgetop cobble occupies a swale, and as you move along, you gain elevation, so the view just gets better and better. The best views are close to a tree island near the cobble's north end, looking into the valleys on either side. Standing on one flank provides a grand west view, and likewise for an east view. There are two large cairns along the cobble's spine that have prominent orange blazes on them, and one has a dead sapling in it used as a pole. Any wide-angle composition must avoid these. The trail passes through the tree island, and on the far side is yet another striking southeast view. This is a good spot for a winter sunrise if you're running late.

Exit the Hall of the Mountain King at 1.32 miles, and immediately begin looking for an opening on the right. You come to an amazing ledge view of the King's Chambers at 1.4 miles. This small ledge sits 25 feet above a cobble and provides an unobstructed panorama of Hill Valley, which sits on this side of Chestnut Ridge. Beyond here, pass a large cobble that sags into a hanging draw. It has a good view, but considering what's next, don't bother stopping.

You arrive at a blue-blazed side trail and trail register at 1.5 miles. Here the Standing Stone Trail turns right to drop off the ridge. Follow the blue blazes through an area of tight undergrowth, and arrive at the Throne Room at 1.6 miles. Proceed into the boulders for several dozen yards, and set up below and to the right of a small tree island. This position has a nearly 180° field of view and looks at a hill-filled valley where the Juniata River meanders south from Lewistown before turning west to slice through Jacks Mountain at Mount Union.

This extraordinary view is the best the Standing Stone Trail has to offer, and it should be savored. Each of the low ridges and hills in the valley to the right has a name, the closest being Chestnut, and the farthest being Mine Bank, which backs up to Blacklog and Cove Mountains beyond. To the northeast, ridges and hills continue beyond Lewistown, and when low fog fills the valley, these high points poke through to render a real-life relief map. Directly ahead in the middle distance is a small reservoir. This is Singers Gap, and Singers Gap Run drops 340 feet through it into Hill Valley.

Looking north over the double ridge of Jack's Mountain, you can make out Juniata Gap between Mount Union and Huntingdon. You can even make out the cobbles flanking a famous hike called Thousand Steps.

Dawn here is sublime in every sense of the word. The white sandstone boulders of the cobble turn from pale blue to rose as the sun hits them. To the west, the sky glows pink over blue as the earth's shadow becomes visible in the atmosphere. Birds begin to announce themselves, and the trees around become alive with them. It is pure magic. Since it's such an easy walk, this mountain view is a must for any photographer. It's on my personal top-five list of the state's best hiking views. I'm sure it'll make yours.

Butler Knob

What I love about the Butler Knob vista is the ease of getting here and the fact that PA 747 and US 522 are hidden by small ridges. Even Augwhick Creek is hidden from view. If you're running late for a Throne Room sunrise, then Butler Knob is the place to go. From the foot of the fire tower, turn right (south) away from cabin 132 on a wide grass trail. In 100 yards, you come to

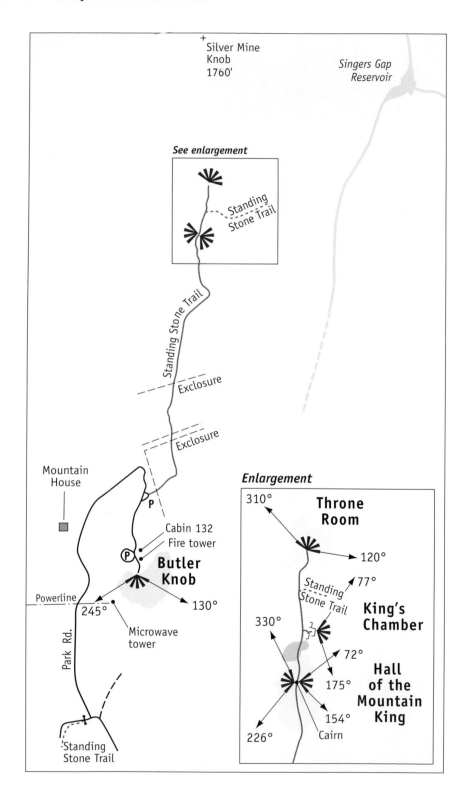

Silver Mine
Knob
1760'

Singers Gap
Reservoir

See enlargement

Standing
Stone Trail

Standing Stone Trail

Exclosure

Exclosure

Mountain
House

P

Cabin 132
Fire tower

Butler
Knob

Powerline

245°

Park Rd.

Microwave
tower

130°

Standing
Stone Trail

Enlargement

310°

**Throne
Room**

120°

Standing
Stone Trail

77°

**King's
Chamber**

330°

72°

175°

**Hall
of the
Mountain
King**

226°

154°

Cairn

Butler Knob. Moving down into the cobble will hide the microwave tower, which is now concealed in the lower right of the frame. High winds required that I weight my tripod legs down with rocks. *Canon EOS Rebel Xs, Tokina 20-35, 1-stop graduate, Kodak E100VS, f/27 @ 2 sec.*

a large, steep cobble. If you want to get a sense of what the Throne Room looks like before you invest the time to hike it, this view should settle the issue. This fabulous location is a south-facing mirror image of the Throne Room, though it lacks the blueberry-picking opportunities. The field of view given above is based on setting up near the trail, but if you descend into the cobble a dozen yards, you can work your way toward the east or west with sufficient exposures to capture summer solstice sunrise. The only issue is a microwave tower below to the right, which can be eliminated by using a normal to slightly longer lens or setting up farther down.

Hike 16 Chimney Rocks, Michaux State Forest

Type: ledge	**Height:** 1,789 feet
Rating: 4	**Best times:** sunrise through midmorning
GPS: 39° 49.143′N, 77° 28.249′W	**Difficulty:** moderate
Faces: 110°	**Distance:** 5.2 miles
Field of view: 50° to 160°	**Time:** 2 hours, 45 minutes
Relief: 30 feet	**Elevation change:** 450 feet
Elevation difference: 538 feet	**Best lenses:** 35mm to 100mm

Directions: From the main square in Gettysburg, take US 30 west for 14.9 miles to the traffic light at PA 233 at Caledonia State Park. Turn left onto PA 233 south and proceed 4.3 miles to a T intersection near South Mountain Restoration Center. A small pond will be in front of you. Turn left and drive .3 mile to where a road comes in from the right. Turn right; then make the first left onto the gravel Swift Run Road. Follow Swift Run for 1.6 miles to a large intersection with Rothrock and Snowy Mountain Roads. Snowy Mountain will be gated on your left. Find a place to park so that you don't block the gate. Roadside Valley View Vista sits a couple miles west of the parking area on Oak Road and provides a decent view of Chambersburg. GPS coordinates: 39° 49.650′N, 77° 30.152′W

Hazy Sunrise. Here the thin veil of valley fog picks up the sky's warm glow. This is a tricky location, with no level surfaces. Always be aware of your tripod's placement before you do anything else. *Tachihara 4x5 field camera, 75mm Rodenstock Grandagon f/6.8, 2-stop graduate, 81A warming filter, 4x5 Ready Load holder, Kodak E100VS, f/32 @ 5 sec.*

This woods road hike descends most of the way to the view. If you're hiking in the dark, you don't get a sense of how steep the descent is until you return. Walk around the gate and gently climb for .5 mile to where a road breaks to the left at a Y. The left fork dead-ends at a cell tower. Bear right and start the long descent to the view. Cross a pipeline at 1.6 miles. About 50 yards to your left is the Appalachian Trail. Climb slightly, cresting a rise at 1.9 miles. At 2.3 miles, you'll enter a wide grassy spot that looks a

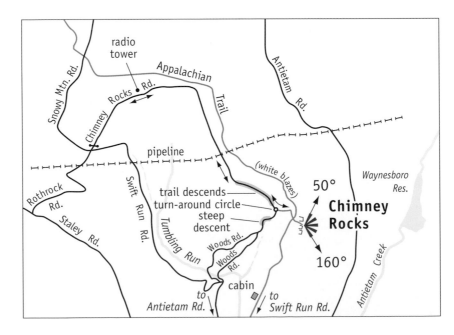

turnaround point. Ahead, the road narrows. On the left, look for a blue blaze on a rock or tree marking the trail to Chimney Rocks. Turn left to follow the blue blazes and gradually ascend, joining the Appalachian Trail at 2.52 miles. In front of you is a sign marking the last 30 yards to Chimney Rocks. Climb the steep rock pile ahead for the view.

This view has some wobbly footing. The rocks are large, eroded slabs that jut upward at odd angles, making it difficult to get a comfortable position. Setting up a tripod can be difficult, as the slabs are rounded such that steel tripod pins don't bite into them well. This is a good spot for rubber tripod feet.

In front of you are the southern end and dam of Waynesboro Reservoir. The north end is hidden by a small hill between you and the water. The view is confined to Antietam Creek valley, in which the reservoir sits. The far side of the valley is the ridge of South Mountain. Immediately below you is Forge Road, and easterly winds carry traffic noises to the vista. What's special about this location is how fog lies in the valley for long periods. The reservoir's cold water keeps fog lingering long after the morning sun has burned it off the rest of the valley.

Hike 17 Buzzard Rocks, Michaux State Forest

Type: cobble	Elevation difference: 456 feet
Rating: 3	Height: 1,642 feet
GPS: 40° 2.269'N, 77° 23.093'W	Best times: early afternoon through sunset
Faces: 250°	Trail: none
Field of view: 230° to 270°	Elevation change: 10 feet
Relief: 10 feet	Best lenses: 50mm to 400mm

Directions: From the main square in Gettysburg, take US 30 west for 14.9 miles to the traffic light at PA 233 at Caledonia State Park. Turn right onto PA 233 north toward Pine Grove Furnace and follow for 10.7 miles. Turn left on Woodrow Road, and take the climbing gravel forest road to an intersection with Ridge Road in 2.8 miles. Cross the perpendicular Ridge Road and turn on Hogshead Road, which lies beyond at a shallow angle to the left. Proceed 1.7 miles to a large parking area on the left.

At some point in the distant past, this view was a local attraction. You can see the remains of a large stone wall confining the parking area. To get the best view, just walk through a gap in the pines on the west side of the lot and find a good rock to stand on. What I like about this view is the way the ridges nest together and overlap. With a long lens, this makes a striking graphic image.

Two creeks cut through the flank of South Mountain to create the interesting pattern before you. The closer is Hairy Springs Hollow, and beyond it is Strohmes Hollow. The ridge or hump in the middle of your view is Tobacco

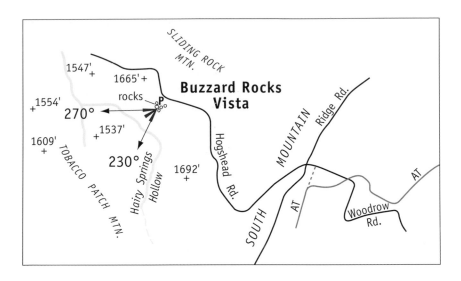

Patch Mountain, the top of which is only 1.4 miles away. The extent of the view is only around 4.5 miles, limited by a 1,700-foot ridgetop just this side of Shippensburg Road.

Hike 18 **Sunset Rocks, Michaux State Forest**

Vista 1

Type: ledge	**Field of view:** 141° to 340°
Rating: 4	**Relief:** 80 feet
GPS: 40° 2.033'N, 77° 19.726'W	**Elevation difference:** 523 feet
Faces: 200°	**Height:** 1,429 feet

Vista 2

Type: ledge	**Field of view:** 140° to 300°
Rating: 4	**Relief:** 90 feet
GPS: 40° 2.005'N, 77° 19.565'W	**Elevation difference:** 421 feet
Faces: 160°	**Height:** 1,350 feet
Best times: early afternoon through sunset	**Time:** 1 hour
Difficulty: difficult; steep climb up Little Rocky Ridge	**Elevation change:** 350 feet
Distance: 1 mile	**Best lenses:** 50mm to 400mm

Directions: From the main square in Gettysburg, take US 30 west 14.9 miles to the traffic light at PA 233 at Caledonia State Park. Turn right onto PA 233 north toward Pine Grove Furnace and proceed 13.3 miles. Turn left on Old Shippensburg Road, following the narrow road until it ends at a dirt pile. If you pass this turn, continue another .1 mile and turn around at the Pine Grove State Park chapel. GPS coordinates: 40° 2.323'N, 77° 19.528'W

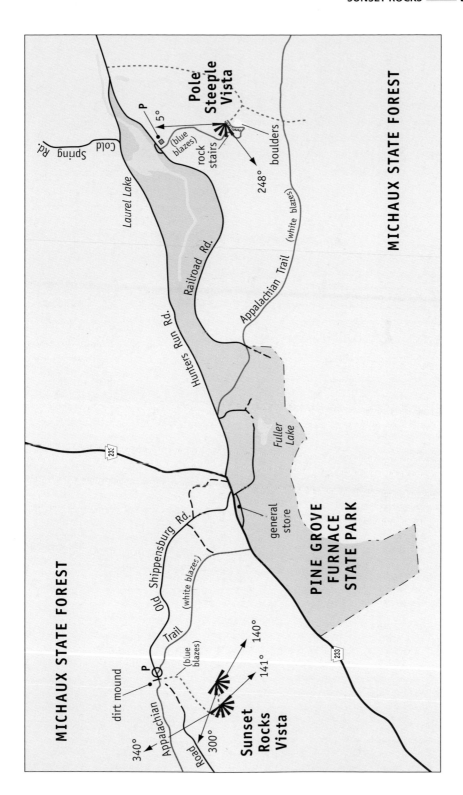

MICHAUX STATE FOREST

Cold Spring Rd.

Laurel Lake

P
5°
(blue blazes)
rock stairs
Pole Steeple Vista
boulders
248°

Railroad Rd.

Hunters Run Rd.

Appalachian Trail (white blazes)

MICHAUX STATE FOREST

23?

Old Shippensburg Rd.

Fuller Lake

general store

PINE GROVE FURNACE STATE PARK

(white blazes)

Trail

233

dirt mound
P
(blue blazes)
140°
141°
Appalachian
300°
340°
Sunset Rocks Vista

Road

MICHAUX STATE FOREST

From the parking area, walk a few dozen yards along the white-blazed Appalachian Trail until you see a footbridge to your right and a sign in a tree directly ahead noting the blue-blazed Sunset Rocks Loop Trail. Bear left and continue along the blue-blazed trail, which climbs more steeply the higher you go up Little Rocky Ridge. At the ridgetop, turn left and go about 80 yards to two rocky vistas that look out on a 140° view of Mountain Creek Valley and Piney Mountain. The trailhead area was logged in 2002, but the blue-blazed trail is a well-worn path and is easily visible.

The view is dominated by the end of Big Hill on your right and the long valley of Dead Woman Hollow, which PA 233 runs through. About 2.5 miles on the right, along a bearing of 244°, you may see a long line of ledges when the leaves are off. This is an area called Lewis Rocks, and it sits on the private Tumbling Run Game Reserve. The ledges may look nice from your vantage, but they aren't very good to photograph from. Following that ridgeline, you'll note that the edge softens the farther southwest you look. This is an area known as Big Flat.

Problematic for this view is the shape of the rocks, which tilt upward with the slabs standing almost on edge. It can be frustrating to get a comfortable perch for a tripod when the only workable flat area is about the size of a shoebox. To return to your car, simply reverse your route.

Hike 19 Pole Steeple, Michaux State Forest

Type: Cliff	**Height:** 1,251 feet
Rating: 5	**Best times:** midmorning through sunset
GPS: 40° 1.966'N, 77° 16.004'W	**Difficulty:** moderate
Faces: 300°	**Distance:** 1.4 miles
Field of view: 248° to 5°	**Time:** 1 hour
Relief: 60 feet	**Elevation change:** 530 feet
Elevation difference: 477 feet	**Best lenses:** 20mm to 100mm

Directions: From the main square in Gettysburg, take US 30 west for 14.9 miles to the traffic light at PA 233 at Caledonia State Park. Turn right onto PA 233 north toward Pine Grove Furnace, and follow for 13.5 miles to a Y intersection at the Pine Grove Furnace park office. Bear right onto Hunters Run Road (SR 3008). (This road is called Hunters Run on all maps but the park map, which calls it Pine Grove Road.) Proceed for 2.2 miles, passing Laurel Lake on your right. At the lake's end, make a hard right onto the first road you find, Railroad Bed Road. Follow it for .3 mile to a large parking area signed for Pole Steeple. GPS coordinates: 40° 2.304'N, 77° 16.195'W

Sunset at Pole Steeple. Note how the sky's warm glow is picked up by the rocks? Heavy summer haze typically ruins sunset shots, but with a nice fore-ground, you can still get good photos. I had to politely ask a few people to move from the edge, and then thanked them profusely when I was done. *Tachihara 4x5 field camera, 150mm Schneider Symmar f/5.6, 2-stop graduate, 81B warming filter, 4x5 Ready Load holder, Kodak E100VS, f/32 @ 5 sec.*

Pole Steeple is my favorite vista in Michaux. The trail is very well marked with blue blazes and is heavily used. I almost hate to say you can't miss it, but you really can't. Cross the road and follow the blue-blazed trail uphill. There's a cabin on your right, so please keep the noise down if you intend to shoot at first light. In the first .3 mile, the trail gains 300 feet before bearing right and leveling off for a short distance. Near .4 mile, it curves left and climbs briskly to the base of the cliff at .6 mile. Here you're given a choice of ascents to the top of Pole Steeple. For the adventurous, when the base of the cliff is in sight, continue straight up an enormous fissure that acts like a narrow staircase for a fun hand-over-hand 60-foot climb. If you're not up for a climb, continue following the blue blazes around the back of the cliff, going through a small boulder field to get to the cliff. I actually prefer this route, because you don't get the view until the last few steps.

Pole Steeple provides a wonderful view of Laurel Lake, and with a pair of binoculars, you can make out Sunset Rocks to your left 3.4 miles away. This is a perfect sunset vista. The only problem is that because it's so popular, it can be crowded on summer evenings. If you get to the view early enough, though, you can pick your spot.

Because the cliffs are split by the central fissure, you can get shots using the cliffs to frame one side of an image. There will be canoes and boats on Laurel Lake any weekend when the lake is ice-free. Look for a bright yellow or red one to shoot with a long lens.

The gray to pinkish quartzite rocks you're standing on were a muddy beach or marine sandbar some 600 million years ago. Bradford Van Diver's book *Roadside Geology of Pennsylvania* has a terrific description of how Pole Steeple was formed. The rocks tilt sharply upward at the cliff edge, making it difficult to stand. This is the edge of a large thrust fault. You're on the side that has been thrust upward. At the cliff base, look for highly polished rock faces. These rocks were part of the fault's slip face and were polished by the fault's terrific pressure and movement.

Hike 20 Three Square Hollow, Tuscarora State Forest

Type: ridge	**Elevation difference:** 1,162 feet
Rating: 5	**Height:** 1,804 feet
GPS: 40° 12.875'N, 77° 32.901'W	**Best times:** sunrise through late afternoon
Faces: 140°	**Trail:** none
Field of view: 90° to 192°	**Elevation change:** none
Relief: 20 feet	**Best lenses:** 20mm to 300mm

Directions: From the PA Turnpike (I-76) interchange at Carlisle, exit onto US 11 south (North Hanover Street) and drive into Carlisle. In 3 miles, turn right onto West High Street to follow US 11 south, PA 641, south and PA 74 west. In 1 mile, US 11 bears left at Ritner Highway and PA 641 turns right onto Newville Road. Turn right onto PA 641/Newville Road, and follow it out of town. In 20.4 miles, at the town of Newburg, turn right onto North High Street (SR 4005). As you pass out of the town limit, it changes names to Three Square Hollow Road (if you pass PA 696, you went one block too far). In 2.1 miles, pass PA 997 and then the turnpike, and at 2.8 miles, you come to a Y intersection where Three Square Hollow Road bears right, Clay Hill Road bears left, and Mitchell Lane turns left. Bear left onto Clay Hill and begin a slow climb, crossing into forestlands in 2 miles. After one switchback turn, you arrive at the view in 3.6 miles.

This is incredible roadside mountain view rivals nearby Flat Rock. Looking down on Cumberland Valley and the small town of Newburg, the 102° field of view seems to be never-ending. You can make out trucks on the turnpike and even the creek-sculpted western flank of South Mountain nearly 16 miles away. If you look very carefully, you can make out the thin ribbon of I-81 13 miles away. The best thing going is a gorgeous white barn sitting at 127°. Even though it's a long-lens shot, on a clear day it'll be keeper for sure.

Hike 21 Doubling Gap, Tuscarora State Forest

Type: ridge	**Elevation difference:** 1,132 feet
Rating: 4	**Height:** 2,030 feet
GPS: 40° 17.189'N, 77° 28.238'W	**Best times:** early morning through late afternoon
Faces: 127°	**Trail:** none
Field of view: 70° to 184°	**Elevation change:** none
Relief: 10 feet	**Best lenses:** 50mm to 200mm

Directions: From the PA Turnpike (I-76) interchange at Carlisle, exit onto US 11 south (North Hanover Street) and drive into Carlisle. In 3 miles, turn right onto West High Street to follow US 11 south, PA 641 south, and PA 74 west. In 1 mile, US 11 bears left at Ritner Highway and PA 641 turns right onto Newville Road. Turn right onto PA 641 and follow it out of town. In 10.9 miles, at the town of Newville, turn right onto PA 233 north. Follow for 12.6 miles, passing Colonel Denning State Park and going over the top of Blue Mountain at Doubling Gap; then make a hard left onto Laurel Run Road. After 6.2 miles, turn right onto Bower Mountain Road. *Warning:* This is a drivable trail that requires high clearance—do not attempt this steep, rocky road in a passenger car. Ascend the steep switchback road for 1.7 miles to Doubling Gap Overlook on the right.

If you don't camp, you now have a good reason in state forest campsite 108, which sits opposite the view. This wonderful spot on Bower Mountain would be the perfect place for a steaming mug of coffee on a crisp fall morning. To the left, you can see all of Sheaffer Valley and Laurel Run, and to the right, you can make out the ridge where Flat Rock sits atop a 6-mile-long W-shaped fold in Blue Mountain. Visible beyond are South Mountain and Michaux State Forest, nearly 20 miles away across Cumberland Valley.

Hike 22 **Flat Rock, Tuscarora State Forest**

Type: ledge	**Height:** 1,987 feet
Rating: 5	**Best times:** sunrise through sunset
GPS: 40° 15.271'N, 76° 24.835'W	**Difficulty:** difficult; steep climbs
Faces: 170°	**Distance:** 4.3 miles
Field of view: 100° to 245°	**Time:** 2 hours, 30 minutes
Relief: 40 feet	**Elevation change:** 1,300 feet
Elevation difference: 1,412 feet	**Best lenses:** 17mm to 100mm

Directions: From the PA Turnpike (I-76) interchange at Carlisle, exit onto US 11 south (North Hanover Street) and drive into Carlisle. In 3 miles, turn right onto West High Street to follow US 11 south, PA 641 south, and PA 74 west. In 1 mile, US 11 bears left at Ritner Highway and PA 641 turns right onto Newville Road. Turn right onto PA 641, and follow it out of town. In 10.9 miles, at the town of Newville, turn right onto PA 233 north. Follow for 8.3 miles, and turn right into Colonel Denning State Park. Make the first right after the visitor center, and descend a steep and narrow road toward the campground. Park at the nature trail loop, with a small amphitheater on the right. GPS coordinates: 40° 16.790'N, 77° 25.127'W

Flat Rock is one of the best mountain views in all of Pennsylvania, and as such, there has to be a price to pay for such an amazing view. In this case, it's a trail so steep that it's difficult to keep your boot heels grounded. From the parking area, walk through the small nature center and cross a footbridge over Doubling Gap Run. In about 100 feet, climb a set of stairs and follow the red-blazed trail through an open woodland.

Looking uphill through the woods, you can see broken views of the ridge, which you'll climb twice. At .1 mile, the trail bears right, away from a creek shed that's been on your left. Then at .2 mile, it drops into and then climbs out of a stream channel. Just beyond, join a woods road and turn left to start your mountain climb. A sign for Camp Yolijwa marks the turn on the way down. At .4 mile, you come to a springhouse, which provides a convenient stopping point to catch your breath. After a short level section, begin climbing again. As you progress, the trail becomes more heavily eroded and the footing tricky.

Finally at 1.1 miles, things level off at a six-point trail intersection called the Wagon Wheel. Proceed straight ahead on the now blue-blazed Tuscarora Trail. After a short walk downhill, you pass a shelter on your left. The trail runs a more or less straight line through a large damp area marking the headwaters of Wildcat Run, which you'll cross at 1.6 miles. If you stop and look around, you'll note that you're surrounded by ridges on three sides. You're in a large bowl formed by a vast W-shaped fold in Blue Mountain. Waggoner Gap to the east is one end of the W, and where PA 233 crosses the ridge to your north is the other. This feature, 3 miles tall by 6 miles wide, was created by immense forces that resulted when several smaller continents crashed together to form the supercontinent of Pangaea nearly 300 million years ago.

Before Leaf-Out. My wife, Diane, sits patiently while I make a few handheld shots for the record. *Canon EOS Digital Rebel, Tokina 20–35, polarizer, ISO200 setting, f/8 @ ¹/60 sec.*

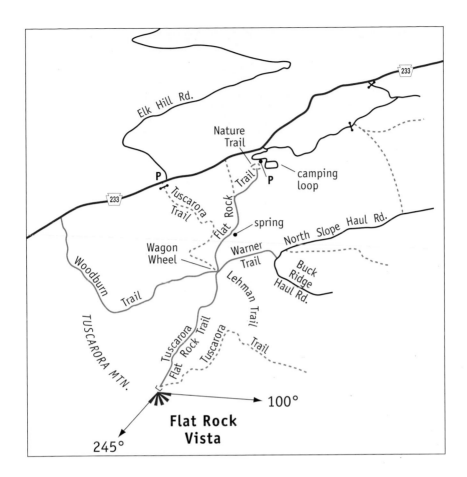

As you continue through the bowl of Wildcat Hollow, the ridge ahead doesn't look all that tall—that is, until you start your final climb and discover you have another 400 vertical feet to go. At 2.1 miles, you top out near a USGS benchmark noting an elevation of 1,919 feet. Make a quick descent to a stone platform overlooking the beautiful Cumberland Valley.

Isn't the view stunning? To the right, some small trees are slowly encroaching on the view and at some point will block the southwest exposure. A cobble below and to the left provides a decent view as well. The ridge on the horizon beyond is South Mountain, part of the Michaux State Forest, which is 15 miles away. Three things need to be considered when composing an image: a barn with a shiny metal roof at 140°, a sand mine west of the Michaux at 142°, and another, larger barn with a shiny metal roof at 182°. When the sun is low in the sky, none of these will be an issue, but during the middle of a clear day, these bright spots will spoil a photograph. If you're shooting digital, play around with a panoramic sequence of images and then stitch them together on a computer. To return to your car, reverse your route.

Hike 23 Waggoner's Gap Hawk Watch

Type: cobble	**Height:** 1,555 feet
Rating: 5	**Best times:** sunrise through late afternoon
GPS: 40° 16.634'N, 76° 16.593'W	**Difficulty:** easy
Faces: 15° and 180°	**Distance:** 200 yards
Fields of view: north from 345° to 45°, south from 140° to 220°	**Time:** 5 minutes
Relief: 20 feet	**Elevation change:** 50 feet
Elevation difference: 1,100 feet	**Best lenses:** 35mm to 90mm

Directions: From the PA Turnpike (I-76) interchange at Carlisle, exit onto US 11 south (North Hanover Street) and drive into Carlisle. In 3 miles, turn right onto West High Street to follow US 11 south, PA 641 south, and PA 74 west. In three blocks, turn right onto North College Street, passing through the Dickinson College campus to follow PA 74 west. In six blocks, PA 74 turns left at B Street. In 8.4 miles, PA 74 crosses over the top of Blue Mountain at a large concrete tower. Descend 200 yards to a parking area on the right. (In winter, park at the ridge crest near a set of radio and cell towers because the parking area below can be iced over.) GPS coordinates: 40° 16.678'N, 76° 16.612'W

The Audubon Society has a spectacular 20-acre property atop Blue Mountain that it uses as a hawk watch. From the parking area below the ridge, follow the short orange-blazed trail to the ridgetop cobble. From the winter parking area atop the ridge, quickly scamper across PA 74 and walk about 30 yards up a gated road. Turn left onto an unblazed footpath, which then swings right toward the ridgetop cobble, arriving at the view in less than 100 yards.

Views to the north and south are spectacular. Of the two, the south view is better. I've been driving over this ridge for years but never bothered to stop and admire the view until I started this project. What a mistake! Sunrise from here is well worth the effort, as are winter sunsets. Carlisle is only 6 miles away. It was difficult to make out through the ground haze, but at twilight it is a shining beacon of light on the horizon.

During holiday visits to see my in-laws, I like to venture out before dawn on Christmas Day. This was my Christmas dawn location for 2005, and in the years I've engaged in my little tradition, I've never seen another soul—which is why Ron Freed's warm greeting took me by total surprise. He was chopping away ice from atop the cobble to make it safe for Audubon's bird-counting teams. After we talked for a while, a few more hardy souls arrived, bundled heavily against the cold. It was a splendid morning.

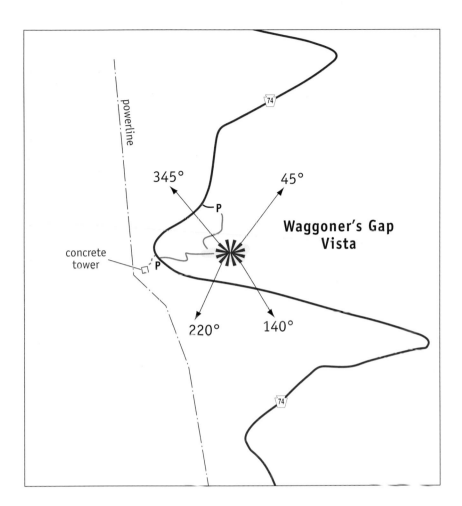

345°

45°

P

Waggoner's Gap
Vista

concrete
tower   P

220°   140°

powerline

Hike 24 Prayer Rock, Mifflin County

Type: ridge	**Elevation difference:** 1,181 feet
Rating: 5	**Height:** 1,900 feet
GPS: 40° 32.624'N, 77° 45.464'W	**Best times:** sunrise through sunset
Faces: 325° and 144°	**Trail:** none
Fields of view: 290° to 360° and 94° to 194°	**Elevation change:** none
Relief: 10 feet	**Best lenses:** 50mm to 175mm

Directions: From the intersection of PA 305 and PA 655 south of Bellville, take PA 655 south for .9 mile and turn left onto Wills Road (SR 4007), following signs for US 522. The road makes a sweeping right. At .4 mile, make the first left to continue on Wills Road, which turns into Front Mountain Road. In 1.6 miles, bear left onto Jacks Mountain Road and climb Jacks Mountain. In 2.9 miles, you come to a large parking area and a small brick shrine atop the ridge.

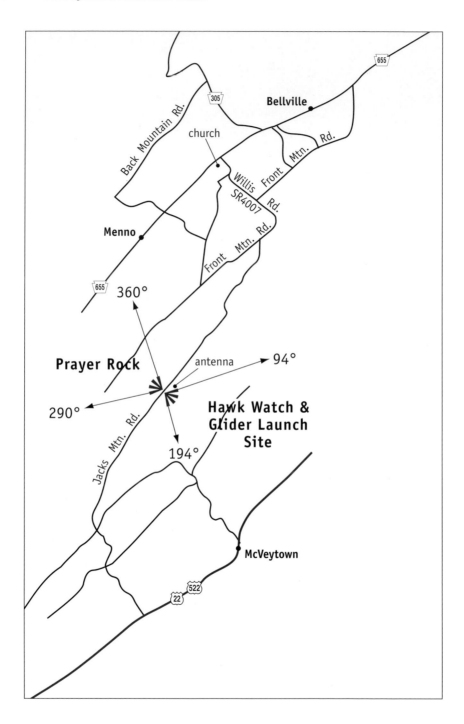

Frosty Dawn at Prayer Rock. Lens flare was murder, so I decided to shoot down the valley, keeping the sun well out of the frame. The sidelighting accentuates the ridges, giving depth to the image. *Tachihara 4x5 field camera, 150mm Schneider Symmar f/5.6, polarizer, 2-stop graduate, 81A warming filter, 6x7 roll film back, Kodak E100VS, f/32 @ 5 sec.*

Also called Jacks Mountain Hawk Watch, this ridge-crest parking area is known locally as Prayer Rock because of the brick shrine on the road's west side. The west side has a great view of Big Valley and the farms below. Although the foreground isn't well maintained, it's clean enough to allow for normal lens compositions.

The east side is much better, with a very impressive wide field of view. This side is also well maintained because it's used as a hang glider launch site, which is simply hard to believe. I had a chance to speak to some pilots at the Tuscarora Mountain launch site on US 30, who told me they just nuzzle up to the guard rail and then take two big steps over the edge to get airborne. I asked, "What if it takes three steps?" Their deadpan response was "Then you've got a big problem."

Sunrise is a must-shoot at any time of year. The widely spaced farms are mostly Amish, so there aren't a lot of security lights fouling the middle ground at twilight. And because the sun doesn't crest the far ridge until almost 15 minutes after sunrise, the bright sky turns off what few lights there are. The low ridges dividing the valley are Church, Middle, and Front Ridges, and they hide the Juniata River from view. If you're running too late to shoot sunrise at Stone Mountain Hawk Watch, which is across the valley to the west, then this is a good backup location.

Hike 25 Sausser's Stone Pile, Standing Stone Trail, Rothrock State Forest

Stone Mountain Hawk Watch

Type: ridge	**Field of view:** 310° to 15° and 70° to 210°
Rating: 5	**Relief:** 10 feet
GPS: 40° 34.306′N, 77° 49.599′W	**Elevation difference:** 1,385 feet
Faces: 340° and 140°	**Height:** 2,184 feet

Sausser's Stone Pile

Type: cobble	**Field of view:** 270° to 15°
Rating: 5	**Relief:** 10 feet
GPS: 40° 34.643′N, 77° 49.316′W	**Elevation difference:** 1,361 feet
Faces: 320°	**Height:** 2,057 feet
Best times: sunrise through sunset	**Time:** 45 minutes
Difficulty: easy; lots of rock hopping	**Elevation change:** 50 feet
Distance: 1.4 miles	**Best lenses:** 17mm to 400mm

Directions: From the visitor center in Greenwood Furnace State Park, turn right onto PA 305 north, and then left into the campground entrance. Make the next left on the gravel Turkey Hill Road. In 5.3 miles, turn left onto Allensville Road and begin climbing Stone Mountain. Bear left at Flat Road and again at Martin Road, and continue climbing. In 2 miles, you come to a switchback with a pullout view. Where the road crosses the ridge, park at the apex of the turn. GPS coordinates: 40° 34.147′N, 77° 49.734′W

Below the parking area is the Allensville Road vista, which faces northwest. It's a nice view and makes for quick work. The only problem is that cars passing downhill usually kick up quite a bit of dust.

From the parking area, walk north along the ridge on an unmarked but clearly visible rocky footpath. The trail rises to the top of a rock pile in 100 yards. Bearing slightly left, move to the back of the rock pile and begin looking for orange blazes downslope and ahead through the trees. There is a brown sign marking the Standing Stone Trail. Left takes you down to Allensville Road and ahead to Stone Mountain Hawk Watch and Sausser's Stone Pile.

Proceed ahead, following the orange-blazed trail along the ridge crest. In .2 mile, the wooden hawk watch platform comes into view. The trail passes to the left of the platform. I find it easier to rock-hop the more open ridge crest. You'll arrive at the splendid viewing platform at .23 mile. The view is a true 360°, but photographically, the best view is to the east, looking down into Big Valley. This is a tremendous sunrise location.

The view northeast is infinite, but I found it difficult to get a good shot looking that way. It does work somewhat, however, when the lights of Bellville and Reedville twinkle in late twilight. I recommend using a long lens to isolate the red barns below. You can easily make out Prayer Rock (Jacks Mountain Hawk Watch) 4 miles away along a bearing of 129°.

Even over this short distance, the rocks have probably been a tad frustrating. Bearing in mind that you probably have boots on, how would you react to five kids flitting around without shoes? When I came to shoot sunset at

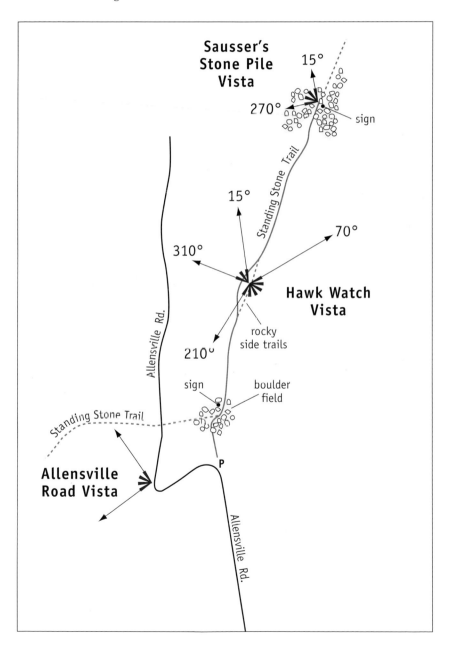

Happy Valley Sunset. It's very windy here, so a low setup is mandatory. *Canon EOS Digital Rebel, Tokina 20–35, polarizer, 2-stop graduate, ISO100 setting, f/22 @ 2.5 sec.*

Sausser's Stone Pile, an Amish family showed up with a picnic dinner, and none of the kids had shoes on. Talk about a sturdy bunch of youngsters!

Continuing along, the rocky Standing Stone Trail arrives at the wide west-facing cobble of Sausser's Stone Pile at .7 mile. When I got here, my first reaction was "Wow!" Spanning 115° this view of Stone Valley is amazing, and the deep cobble eliminates foreground problems. Any place you set up will provide a publishable photo. A farm to the right has a pole shed with a shiny white roof, which will remain lit until about thirty minutes before sunset. If you take care of how it's placed in the frame, it shouldn't be an issue.

One other concern is the ever-present wind. The stone pile sits in a low swale, and breezes tend to accelerate through the gap. I found that a mild tree-shaking breeze hit me with quite a bit of force. I recommend setting up low.

Hike 26 # Spruce Knob, Mid State Trail, Rothrock State Forest

Vista 1

Type: cobble	**Field of view:** visto
Rating: 2	**Relief:** 20 feet
GPS: 40° 36.180'N, 78° 6.995'W	**Elevation difference:** 823 feet
Faces: 310°	**Height:** 1,673 feet

Vista 2

Type: cobble	**Field of view:** visto
Rating: 4+	**Relief:** 10 feet
GPS: 40° 36.391'N, 78° 6.875'W	**Elevation difference:** 1,130 feet
Faces: 285°	**Height:** 1,980 feet

Spruce Knob

Type: cobble	**Field of view:** 210° to 300°
Rating: 5+	**Relief:** 20 feet
GPS: 40° 36.465'N, 78° 6.869'W	**Elevation difference:** 1,129 feet
Faces: 265°	**Height:** 2,069 feet
Best times: late morning through sunset	**Time:** 2 hours, 30 minutes
Difficulty: strenuous; steeps climbs	**Elevation change:** 1,420 feet
Distance: 3.4 miles	**Best lenses:** 17mm to 100mm

Directions: From the intersection of US 22 and PA 26 west of Huntingdon, take US 22 west for 5.7 miles to PA 305 near Alexandria. Turn right onto PA 305 north and proceed toward Alexandria for .5 mile, crossing the river; then turn left onto Main Street (SR 4014). Follow Main for .6 mile, and turn right onto SR 4004 toward Barree. Cross a railroad, and in about 2 miles cross another railroad. Immediately after, SR 4004 turns left to cross a bridge over the Little Juniata River. After the river crossing, turn left onto Mountain Road for .6 mile to where it dead-ends in a large parking area. GPS coordinates: 40° 35.541'N, 78° 6.675'W

The parking area can be crowded on weekends, not with hikers, but with fly fishers. This wide and slow-running section of the Little Juniata River is very popular with anglers, who arrive in numbers in the early part of the day. That's OK—this is a sunset shoot, and they'll all have left by the time you arrive.

Begin by locating the orange-blazed Mid State Trail (MST), which is marked by a sign, near the middle of the parking lot. You start climbing right away on a grade that in many places doesn't allow you to keep your boot heels down. Ever upward you climb, until at .6 mile, you pop out onto an old rail grade where the MST turns left. This delightfully level section affords broken views of the valley to the west. At .91 mile, turn right and begin another climb steeper than the first. Fortunately it's short, ending at 1 mile. Here you'll find a small cobble with a narrow northwesterly view. Blazes from here on are difficult to find, and the rocky trail is indistinct in places, making for slow progress on your return.

The MST continues to climb again, although not as steeply. Rocks become more troublesome as you climb, indicating that perhaps there's some kind of opening to the left. A good one is found at 1.56 miles just off the trail. This southwest view is incredible. Although the cobble isn't large, its steepness and shape make it a nice backup shooting location if you can't get to Spruce Knob in time for sunset. If time isn't an issue, dally here, given that this is just a warm-up for what's next.

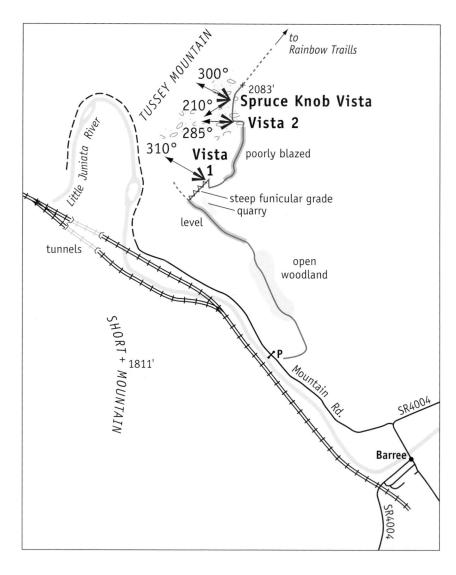

Tree Glow at Spruce Knob. This is the toughest location I've ever hauled gear to, but it's worth every bump and bruise. *Tachihara 4x5 field camera, 75mm Rodenstock Grandagon f/6.8, 2-stop graduate, 81A warming filter, 6x7 roll film back, Kodak E100VS, f/32 @ 6 sec*

Return to the MST and continue uphill. About 75 yards farther, note a large opening on the left. In a few more yards, the MST crests Tussey Mountain at a huge ridge-hugging cobble. This is Spruce Knob. This cobble is more than 200 yards wide and spills down the mountain quite a way. Explore all of it, since the MST just nips the south edge of it. In fact, the view you passed 100 yards back was part of this cobble.

As you walk out into the rock field, the view just gets better and better. If you turn left and work away from the MST, the view becomes overwhelming. I think this is the best view in all of Pennsylvania. To the left, across the gap, the continuation of Tussey Mountain looms large, yet in the left middle distance, the point of Cove Mountain looks like model train scenery. The wide valley before you is Sinking Valley, which seems almost limitless. What makes this view so special is how Brush and Cove Mountains hide Tyrone, Bellwood, and Altoona, which sits 16 miles away along the view's primary sight line. All are invisible, hidden by the ridges.

On my first trip here, it was hazy, hot, and humid. Shooting conditions were less than ideal, and I wasn't prepared to stay for sunset. With less than an hour of daylight left, I headed back to my truck. That's when I began to notice that large rocks near the trail had recently been overturned. Upended rocks are a sure sign of bear activity, and rocks that have been moved within the last hour mean that you should be very attentive. I heard rustling downhill on my left and froze, looking into the deep shadows cast by the setting sun. At that moment, a 200-pound female black bear bolted for a thicket not 30 yards away. With clear sight lines, I got a good look at her during her headlong dash, and the question that popped into my mind was "Where's the cubs?"

That question answered itself a few seconds later, when I hear a loud rustling down a steep slope to my right. Kneeling behind a tree, I tried to spy the cub, but it saw me first, made a little bleating cry, then flew downhill, leaping into a tree and climbing it in seconds. I hadn't known cubs could move that quickly. While all this was rattling around in my brain, it dawned on me that I was between a sow and her cub. Just because black bears tend to be shy and skittish doesn't mean they aren't protective of their young. Even though Mom had bolted away from her cub, she might soon react to its weak cry. My only solution was to look menacing and move quickly. The former I did badly, but the latter I did rather well. Even though this kind of thing gets the heart racing, such encounters are rare and should be treasured. Few people ever see bears outside of zoos, and I count myself many times lucky for having seen more than a dozen in creating this guide.

As an alternate route, Spruce Knob can be accessed from the blue-blazed Rainbow Trail at Colerain Road. This short but very steep trail of fist-size rock scree climbs the ridge 600 feet to bring you to the orange-blazed MST. Turning right (south) gets you to the knob. The MST is poorly blazed and unmaintained for the 1.5 miles to the knob. It should be attempted only by those with more than casual hiking experience. I've done it in the dark and can say it is the most frustrating trail in Pennsylvania.

Hike 27 Indian Overlook, Rothrock State Forest

Type: cliff	**Height:** 1,543 feet
Rating: 4	**Best times:** afternoon through sunset
GPS: 40° 37.461'N, 78° 6.351'W	**Difficulty:** easy
Faces: 345°	**Distance:** .4 mile
Field of view: 300° to 30°	**Time:** 45 minutes
Relief: 100 feet	**Elevation change:** 175 feet
Elevation difference: 700 feet	**Best lenses:** 35mm to 90mm

Directions: From the intersection of US 22 and PA 26 west of Huntingdon, take US 22 west for 7.9 miles to PA 45/350 north. In .7 mile, turn right onto PA 45 north proper. As you make the turn, look at the mountain on your right for a massive cobble heading Spruce Knob (Hike 26). In 4.7 miles, you pass through Spruce Creek and the village of Colerain. Turn right onto Colerain Road for the creekside Colerain Picnic Area. After you cross Spruce Creek, turn left to continue on Colerain Road and cross into Rothrock State Forest. After 2.3 miles of climbing, which includes one switchback turn with an impressive view, you come to a parking area on the left with several white posts. If you reach a Y intersection of Colerain and Brady Roads, you went a couple hundred yards too far. GPS coordinates: 40° 37.342'N, 78° 6.244'W

Indian Overlook. A quick hike to a nice spot. *Canon EOS Digital Rebel, Tokina 20–35, polarizer, 1-stop graduate, ISO400 setting, f/8 @ ¹/100 sec.*

This short descending hike brings you to a delightful view overlooking the village of Colerain and Sinking Valley. Head downhill on the blue-blazed Ice Cave Gap Trail, starting off with a pleasant descent along a wide woods road. In the last 100 yards, climb up over a steep berm to get to the view. When you come over the berm's top, you'll see a stone fence with a narrow gap that allows you to get out onto the ledge. Please do so carefully, as this location has had one fatality in recent years.

Sitting nearly 700 feet lower than the Mid State Trail, which is atop the ridge behind you, this ledge feels as if it's hanging over Colerain village. Houses along PA 45 are problematic for a wide-angle shot, so use a normal to long lens here. Spruce Creek sits out of view below, hidden by a tree-lined meander. Near the left limit of view is a gap in the far ridge. This is where the Little Juniata River cuts through Bald Eagle Mountain at Tyrone. This ridge hides all the towns on the west side of it. Indian Overlook is heavily used and has a great many cigarette butts lying around. To shoot any foreground rocks, you'll have to do some extensive gardening and trash picking.

For some additional views, the switchback vista you passed at 40° 36.996′N, 78° 7.372′W provides an impressive 4-rated view and makes for a quick sunset spot. If you continue uphill along Colerain Road for 1.3 miles past the Indian Overlook parking area, you'll arrive at another very impressive roadside view rated 4+ at 40° 37.814′N, 78° 5.272′W. Both are superb

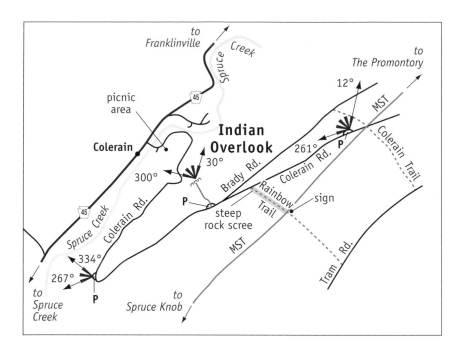

locations for playing with a long lens to isolate farms and interesting shapes within the contoured plowed fields. A third location up and over the ridge crest from Colerain Road is overgrown and unworkable.

Hike 28 **The Promontory, Mid State Trail, Rothrock State Forest**

Type: ridge	**Height:** 2,033 feet
Rating: 3	**Best times:** morning through midday
GPS: 40° 38.895′N, 78° 3.701′W	**Difficulty:** moderate; overgrown trail
Faces: 125°	**Distance:** 1.8 miles
Field of view: 84° to 175°	**Time:** 1 hour, 30 minutes
Relief: 10 feet	**Elevation change:** 160 feet
Elevation difference: 925 feet	**Best lenses:** 35mm to 100mm

Directions: From the intersection of US 22 and PA 26 west of Huntingdon, take US 22 west for 7.9 miles to PA 45/350 north. In .7 mile, turn right onto PA 45 north proper. As you make the turn, look at the mountain on your right for a massive cobble heading Spruce Knob (Hike 26). In 4.7 miles, you pass through Spruce Creek and the village of Colerain. Turn right onto Colerain Road. After you cross Spruce Creek, turn left to continue on Colerain Road and cross into Rothrock State Forest. In 2.4 miles, at a Y intersection of Colerain and Brady Roads, bear left to follow Brady Road. In 3.4 miles, you reach a wide spot with a trail marker on the right for the Brewer Path. GPS coordinates: 40° 39.332′N, 78° 3.251′W

It's surprising how easily the blue-blazed Brewer Path climbs to the top of Tussey Mountain. A steady climb up the amply blazed and well-worn footpath brings you to the Mid State Trail (MST) in .21 mile. Turn right (south) on the orange-blazed MST for the Promontory. At .51 mile, you come to a small gap with a south view. From here to the viewpoint, the MST is poorly maintained, with intermittent blazes and extensive overgrowth crowding the trail. Be prepared to get whacked in the head many times by overhanging branches.

At .9 mile, you reach a ridgetop opening and small cobble with a large cairn marking the viewpoint. Even on a hazy June day, this was a pretty good location. This vista doesn't have a long-range view, but only allows a good look at Diamond Valley and two ridges surrounding it. There are some spindly trees in the foreground, but moving will get them out of view. Although the vista also has northwest exposure, there is no real view in that direction.

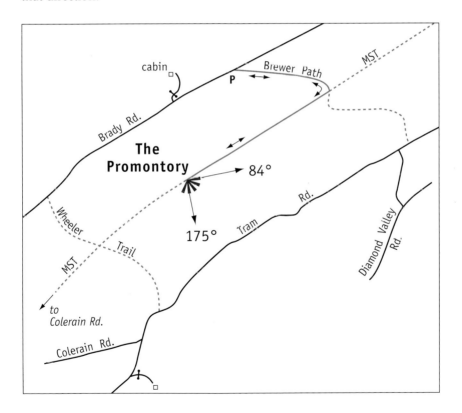

Hike 29 Dave's and Old Pine Vistas, Jackson Trail, Rothrock State Forest

Dave's Vista

Type: cobble	Field of view: 115° to 208°
Rating: 4	Relief: 5 feet
GPS: 40° 43.297'N, 77° 52.926'W	Elevation difference: 823 feet
Faces: 160°	Height: 2,139 feet

Old Pine Vista

Type: ridge	Field of view: 90° to 240°
Rating: 3	Relief: 20 feet
GPS: 40° 43.890'N, 77° 51.468'W	Elevation difference: 1,129 feet
Faces: 165°	Height: 2,109 feet
Best times: midafternoon through sunset	Time: 2 hours
Difficulty: easy; some rocky sections	Elevation change: 150 feet
Distance: 4.8 miles	Best lenses: 35mm to 100mm

Directions: From the intersection of PA 26 and PA 25 in Pine Grove Mills, south of State College, take PA 26 west 2.1 miles to the crest of Tussey Mountain, and park adjacent to the large highway warning sign in the large parking area for Jo Hays Vista. GPS coordinates: 40° 42.984'N, 77° 53.664'W

This level hike on the blue-blazed Jackson Trail, although rocky in places, is a good family outing with youngsters, particularly the first .75-mile section to Dave's Vista. Jo Hays Vista provides a nice view of State College, but I don't find this location to be all that photogenic because of the way the foreground brush is cut back.

Carefully cross PA 26 and walk around the gate. The blue-blazed Jackson Trail begins as a graded woods road. At .12 mile, you come to a cluster of antennas. Bear left, following the blue-blazed road and exiting the antenna field at .21 mile. Here the road begins to fade, becoming more rocky, until at .4 mile you're no longer walking on soil but rock-hopping. Enter a boulder field at .55 mile, leaving a short time later for a large hemlock grove. Just after, you'll find a large cairn and sign for Dave's Vista at .75 mile.

This relatively level cobble is named for David Kaufman, who died in 1997. With 4 acres of boulders, this southwest view makes for an excellent picnic spot. Mountain laurel bushes near the Jackson Trail make for nice foregrounds, and as with all cobbles, where you stand determines the view.

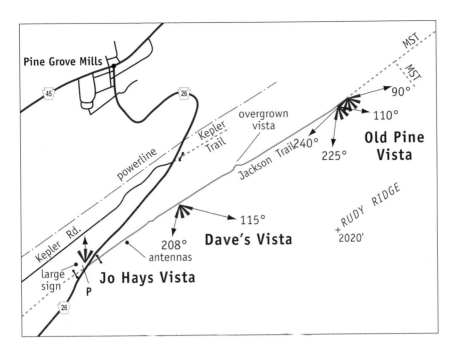

Pine Grove Mills

45

26

overgrown
vista

Kepler
Trail

powerline

Jackson Trail 240°

90°

110°

MST

MST

Old Pine
Vista

225°

115°

208°

antennas

RUDY RIDGE

+
2020'

Kepler Rd.

large
sign

P

Dave's Vista

Jo Hays Vista

26

A few trees within the rocks require that you carefully pick a location. Here it's best toward the left.

Not more than 50 yards after Dave's Vista is another cobble with restricted northwest views. Bypass this and the next viewpoint found at .92 mile. Thankfully you leave the rocks behind at 1 mile for more comfortable hiking. An opening that appears on the right near 1.17 miles affords no view. Rocks return again at 1.22 miles as you climb a short distance onto the shattered spine of Tussey Mountain. At 1.55 miles, you reach a large opening with views to the southwest. It's an OK view, but I wouldn't waste too much time here.

While I was hiking across this cobble's head, a thought occurred to me. I hadn't seen any snakes except for a black king

Blooming Laurel. On a hazy afternoon, I looked around for a foreground to play with and found this blooming mountain laurel. *Canon EOS Digital Rebel, Tokina 20–35, polarizer, ISO400 setting, f/22 @ 1/6 sec.*

snake two days earlier. At that exact moment, a timber rattler let me know it was below my right boot and would appreciate it very much if I didn't step on it. It was in a tight coil, tail up rattling, with its gaze fixed on my legs. Angry rattlesnakes don't sound anything like what you hear on TV or in the movies. In real life, their sound is more of buzz, like a thousand angry bees. This one was about 3 feet long with a charcoal black head. We took to staring at each other across several feet of open space. It won our little contest, so I diverted around, and the snake slowly uncoiled to continue sunning itself on a rock.

Another cobble with decent views is found at 2.15 miles, but it's not photogenic at all. Shortly after, you cross the head of another cobble, followed by heavy overgrowth crowding the trail. Finally, at 2.30 miles, you enter a very big ridge-hugging cobble. From here to the true view of Old Pine Vista, you'll be along the spine of this cobble. Views all along the ridge are extensive and wide. The best view is toward the far end of the cobble, about 40 yards from where it enters the woods again, but the 2,004-foot-tall hump of Rudy Ridge makes it difficult to get a photograph. There are no other views from here to the Mid State Trail junction, so it's best to turn around and head back to your car.

Hike 30 Indian Wells, Mid State Trail, Rothrock State Forest

Type: cobble	**Height:** 2,397 feet
Rating: 4+	**Best times:** sunrise through midmorning, late afternoon
GPS: 40° 43.847′N, 77° 46.921′W	**Difficulty:** easy
Faces: 105°	**Distance:** 1.8 miles
Field of view: 80° to 175°	**Time:** 1 hour, 30 minutes
Relief: 10 feet	**Elevation change:** 80 feet
Elevation difference: 576 feet	**Best lenses:** 17mm to 400mm

Directions: From the intersection of PA 26 and PA 25 in Pine Grove Mills, south of State College, take PA 26 west for 3 miles, passing over the crest of Tussey Mountain and Jo Hays Vista. Turn left onto Pine Swamp Road, proceed for 5 miles, and turn left onto Laurel Run Road. In 2.9 miles, make a hard right onto Bear Gap Road and climb a steep hill. Go 1.6 miles, passing Bear Gap Vista, and park in a large parking area on the left just shy of the gated Gettis Road. GPS coordinates: 40° 43.462′N, 77° 47.450′W

Before Dawn. Sky glow will always make foregrounds look better. In this case, the pink of the sky is picked up by the white Tuscarora sandstone of the cobble. *Canon EOS Digital Rebel, Tokina 20–35, 2-stop graduate, 10CC magenta, ISO100 setting, f/8 @ 8 sec.*

There is limited parking adjacent to the trailhead and at Bear Gap Vista, which is why the large parking area up the hill is a better choice. Bear Gap Vista is a very nice spot to linger and take in a northwest view of Laurel Run near Hubler Gap.

From the parking area, walk .2 mile down the road toward Bear Gap Vista and turn right onto the blue-blazed Keith Spring Trail. There'll be an engraved stone marker and a brown sign indicating no bikes allowed on the trail. The trail is level and intersects the orange-blazed Mid State Trail (MST) at a T. Turn left and at .63 mile you'll come to a campsite where the MST turns right. Take the time to look for orange blazes, as there are three unblazed trails exiting the campsite.

Shortly after, the MST climbs slightly through some rocks, and when it arrives at Indian Wells Vista, it turns left to follow the head of the 300-yard-long cobble. The best overall location is near a dead tree with an orange blaze on it. The view into Bear Meadows Natural Area is fantastic. The natural area is a large bowl marking the headwaters area of Sinking Creek, so you can expect ground fog here even when the humidity is low. On my sun-

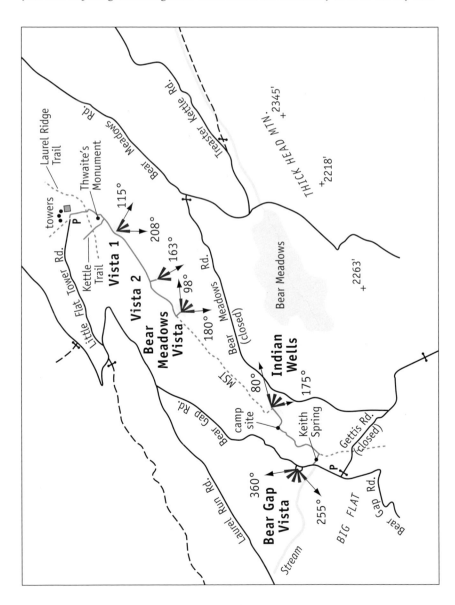

rise shoot, fog formed a thin layer about 10 feet in the air, and dead trees surrounding the meadow reached through it like talons. No matter what focal-length lens you start with, you'll end up using a long lens, because this is certainly the location for it. My longest lens is a 400mm, which when mounted to my digital body has an effective length of 540mm. I shot about 200 frames with it—that's how good a long lens location this is. I recommend that as a follow-up to the long-lens view, you drive around to Treaster Kettle Road and hike into the meadow from the Jean Aram Trail. Just don't forget where the name Bear Meadows comes from.

If you'd like to continue along the MST to Bear Meadows Vista (Hike 31), exit the cobble to the north, following the orange blazes, and arrive at Bear Meadows in 1 mile.

Hike 31 Bear Meadows, Mid State Trail, Rothrock State Forest

Vista 1

Type: cobble	Field of view: 115° to 208°
Rating: 3	Relief: 10 feet
GPS: 40° 44.834'N, 77° 45.464'W	Elevation difference: 597 feet
Faces: 155°	Height: 2,416 feet

Vista 2

Type: cobble	Field of view: visto
Rating: 2	Relief: 10 feet
GPS: 40° 44.572'N, 77° 45.864'W	Elevation difference: 577 feet
Faces: 163°	Height: 2,396 feet

Bear Meadows

Type: cobble	Field of view: 98° to 180°
Rating: 3	Relief: 20 feet
GPS: 40° 44.423'N, 77° 46.122'W	Elevation difference: 598 feet
Faces: 142°	Height: 2,417 feet
Best times: sunrise through midday	Time: 1 hour, 30 minutes
Difficulty: easy; some rocky sections	Elevation change: 30 feet
Distance: 3 miles	Best lenses: 17mm to 400mm

Directions: From the intersection of PA 26 and PA 25 in Pine Grove Mills, south of State College, take PA 26 west for 3 miles, passing over the crest of Tussey Mountain and Jo Hays Vista. Turn left onto Pine Swamp Road, proceed for 5 miles, and turn left onto Laurel Run Road. In 3.9 miles, make a right onto Little Flat Tower Road, and continue to the dead-end parking area under a shady tree. GPS coordinates: 40° 45.115'N, 77° 45.357'W

Following a level section of the Mid State Trail (MST) from Little Flat Tower along the flank of Tussey Mountain, this trail provides three nice views into Bear Meadows Natural Area. Little Flat Tower is one of the few climbable towers in the state, but the view is restricted by spruce trees that are now taller than the tower. Even so, it's a fun little climb as the tower sways pleasantly in the breeze.

Begin by walking away from the radio towers and cabin, heading south along the orange-blazed MST. The route is level and pleasant. In a few yards, it crosses a pole line, and at .12 mile, it intersects the Laurel Ridge Trail. Continue ahead, following orange blazes. In short order, it intersects the Spruce Gap Trail, which joins from the left.

At .3 mile, you come to a monument to Tom Thwaites, the father of many of Pennsylvania's best trails. The Kettle Trail joins at the monument from the left. Continue along the MST, now called the Tom Thwaites Foot Path, passing a trail register and then a campsite on the right. At .47 mile, you reach a signed trail to a view on the left. This fine view looks into Bear Meadows along a bearing of 184°. Trees on the right limit the view of the natural area,

Ground Fog. Notice how the trees reach through the ground fog? This is when you shoot a long lens to isolate graphic patterns and shapes. *Canon EOS Digital Rebel, Tamron 200–400, polarizer, ISO100 setting, f/16 @ ¹/₅ sec.*

however, and Thickhead Mountain limits the range of view. Look around for elaborate and whimsical cairns. If you've brought kids along, grab some rocks and build one of your own.

Return to the MST, turn left, and pass the Fleet Foot Trail to Cool Spring, which joins from the right. At 1 mile, turn left for another signed view. This vista of Bear Meadows is a long-lens shot. Dead tree clutter at the cobble base eliminates the possibility of a quality wide-angle shot. Returning again to the MST, turn left. On the way to the next view, you pass through a burn area on your right. Surrounding the trail are acres of lowbush blueberries, which ripen between the end of June and the beginning of July. This area provides the hungry hiker with a movable feast. Bring a bucket!

You'll come to another signed view trail at 1.43 miles. Again turn left, arriving at the view at 1.5 miles. The trail to the view is nearly overgrown, but the footpath on the ground is clear. Just be prepared to fight through a few mountain laurel bushes to get out into the cobble.

Although this cobble is 150 yards wide, it's not very deep, which makes wide-angle work difficult. Although I'm not a big fan of digital manipulation, this is one shot where I would crop out the foreground, since the view is wide enough to include the meadows and quite a bit of Sinking Creek. The best location is left of a tree island, as the right is fouled by a line of dead trees.

If you'd like to continue along the MST, you will come to Indian Wells Vista (Hike 30) in 1 mile. Otherwise, return to your car and enjoy your fresh-picked mountain blueberries.

Hike 32 Kohler and Long Mountains, Bald Eagle State Forest

Bell's Majestic Vista

Type: ridge	Field of view: 300° to 4°
Rating: 4	Relief: 10 feet
GPS: 40° 49.775′N, 77° 30.551′W	Elevation difference: 778 feet
Faces: 330°	Height: 1,845 feet

Best times: late morning to late afternoon

Pine Swamp Vista

Type: ridge	Field of view: 40° to 120°
Rating: 4	Relief: 25 feet
GPS: 40° 49.938′N, 77° 27.073′W	Elevation difference: 351 feet
Faces: 80°	Height: 1,525 feet

Best times: early morning to midday

Penns View	
Type: ledge	**Field of view:** 315° to 65°
Rating: 3	**Relief:** 40 feet
GPS: 40° 50.553'N, 77° 27.181'W	**Elevation difference:** 716 feet
Faces: 350°	**Height:** 1,726 feet
Best times: late morning to late afternoon	
Trail: none	**Best lenses:** 35mm to 300mm
Elevation change: none	

Directions: Begin this driving tour from the intersection of PA 45 and PA 445 in Millheim northeast of State College.

These three drivable mountain views provide the best available vistas in
this southern section of Bald Eagle State Forest. The Ridge and Valley
Province's arrangement of long, slender ridges separates the forest into three
distinct sections: this one, Thick Mountain to the south, and one centered
around PA 192 south of I-80.

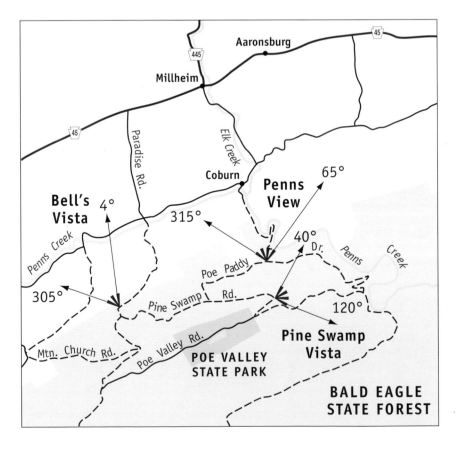

Pine Swamp View. A simple midday shot from a delightful spot. *Tachihara 4x5 field camera, 210mm Schneider Symmar-S f/5.6, polarizer, 2-stop graduate, 6x7 roll film back, Kodak E100VS, f/32 @ 1 sec.*

From the intersection with PA 445, take PA 45 south for 1.5 miles, and turn left onto Paradise Road. In 2.3 miles, you come to Penns Creek and SR 1012. In .5 mile, turn left; then make a hard right onto Siglerville Manheim Pike Road, which starts off as paved but becomes gravel when it enters forestlands. In 2.4 miles, you reach Bell's Majestic Vista on the right. Looking into Zerby Gap and Penn Valley beyond, this is a fine mountain view. Nearby ridges restrict the long-range view, and during fall color, this is a heck of a location.

Continue your drive by making the first left after Bell's Majestic Vista onto Pine Swamp Road, bearing left at 1 mile to remain on Pine Swamp Road. You'll arrive at the next view at 3.5 miles. Situated at the apex of a sharp right turn, Pine Swamp Vista looks out on a series of tightly nested ridges confining Poe Valley. This is a charming little view that lends itself to long-lens graphic shots of overlapping ridges. Try this location in either the morning or the failing light of sunset, when the valley takes on a rosy hue.

Turn around as best you can and head back uphill for 1.3 miles. Turn right onto Poe Paddy Road, looking for a sign for Penns View. In 1.8 miles, you come to a large parking area for Penns View on the left. A note of driving caution: Bald Eagle State Forest has more than 90 miles of motorcycle trails using unmaintained forest roads. Take care when approaching Penns View, as you may encounter a dozen or more fast-moving dirt bikes flying toward you. Also, the road beyond Penns View is a drivable trail that requires a high-clearance vehicle. Do not attempt to descend this road into Poe Paddy State Park unless you have experience on such roads.

Penns View is a sheer ledge formed by a tightly entrenched meander of Penns Creek. Looking directly into the narrow Still House Gap, just out of view is a large valley where Penns, Elk, and Pine Creeks join together. If you're up for a little scramble, you can readily descend from the parking area view to a small ledge in a few feet. Just take care, as loose soil can make for difficult footing in damp conditions. On the view's right side is a large clear-cut on the flank of Woodward Mountain, making wide-angle work difficult. From the lower ledge, a large house is in view. I'd recommend a normal lens on the order of 50mm to get the best compositions. Look for brightly colored rafts or kayaks in Penns Creek offsetting the green background.

To complete your outing, reverse your route back to Millheim.

Hike 33 New Lancaster Valley, Bald Eagle State Forest

Type: ridge	**Elevation difference:** 785 feet
Rating: 4	**Height:** 1,966 feet
GPS: 40° 47.618'N, 77° 18.630'W	**Best times:** morning to late afternoon
Faces: 252°	**Trail:** none
Field of view: 230° to 270°	**Elevation change:** none
Relief: 10 feet	**Best lenses:** 50mm to 200mm

Directions: In the southernmost section of Bald Eagle State Forest, which encompasses Thick Mountain, only one viewpoint is worth your time, and it sits at the head of the canoe-shaped New Lancaster Valley. Begin from Reeds Gap State Park east of Milroy and Locke Mills, heading east along New Lancaster Valley Road (SR 1002) for 7.9 miles, and bear right to continue on the paved road. In .5 mile, you come to a hairpin right-hand turn with a forest road at the beginning. Bear left onto Locust Ridge Road. You'll arrive at the view in 2.2 miles.

Sitting at the head of New Lancaster Valley, this vista offers a unique view of the Seven Mountains region topography. The plateau you're on is about 1,900 feet in elevation, and the ridgetops stand around 2,200 feet. What you see clearly from here is how different an end-on view of the sharp-topped ridges looks compared to a side view from one of the valley roads such as PA 45.

The ridges are made of distinct forms, a flat-topped plateau with a pointy ridge sitting on top, which is created by two different hard stone layers. The canoe shape is formed by a huge fold in Jacks Mountain where it joins Thick Mountain on the right. Behind you, the ridge crests join at a feature called High Top, a long S-shaped fold.

Predawn Glow. The sun rises perpendicular to New Lancaster Valley, which casts deep shadows as soon as the sun gets over the ridges. For morning shooting, you have to work while the sun is below the horizon; otherwise you'll have to wait a couple hours for the valley to fill with light. *Canon EOS Rebel Xs, Tokina 20–35, 2-stop graduate, 10CC magenta, Kodak E100VS, f/27 @ 2 sec.*

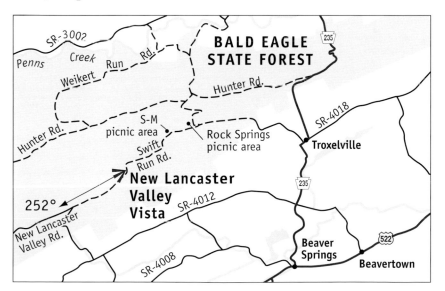

Hike 34 Shriner Mountain, Bald Eagle State Forest

Type: ridge	**Elevation difference:** 467 feet
Rating: 3 to 4	**Height:** 2,105 feet
GPS: 40° 58.394'N, 77° 8.467'W	**Best times:** morning to late afternoon
Faces: 252°	**Trail:** none
Field of view: 240° to 310°	**Elevation change:** none
Relief: 10 feet	**Best lenses:** 50mm to 400mm

Directions: From R.B. Winter State Park west of Lewisburg, take PA 192 east for 1.4 miles. Turn right onto Pine Creek Road just after you exit park lands for forestland. At a T intersection, turn left onto Jones Mountain Road and proceed 3 miles to the view.

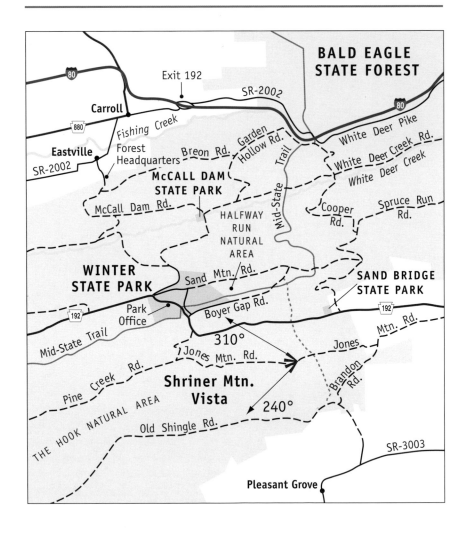

Ridge Patterns. This location is made for extreme telephoto. In this case, the camera's inherent 1.6X magnification makes my 400mm lens act like a 640mm supertelephoto. Exploring patterns like these is great fun. *Canon EOS Digital Rebel, Tamron 200–400, ISO100 setting, polarizer, f/16 @ $^1/_6$ sec.*

This is the only viewpoint I like in the northern section of Bald Eagle State Forest, which lies between PA 45 and I-80. Facing west, it overlooks a series of overlapping ridges and gaps where the Seven Mountains collide. This location is perfect for a graphic image shot after the sun goes down and wisps of fog begin to rise from the narrow valleys.

Hike 35 Fred Woods Trail, Elk State Forest

Sinnemahoning Creek near Mix Run

Vista 1

Type: ridge	**Field of view:** visto
Rating: 3	**Relief:** 10 feet
GPS: 41° 21.247'N, 78° 12.279'W	**Elevation difference:** 1,048 feet
Faces: 280°	**Height:** 1,942 feet

Vista 2

Type: ledge	**Field of view:** 180° to 260°
Rating: 3	**Relief:** 10 feet
GPS: 41° 21.015'N, 78° 12.263'W	**Elevation difference:** 1,045 feet
Faces: 220°	**Height:** 1,939 feet

Vista 3

Type: cobble	**Field of view:** 254° to 304°
Rating: 3	**Relief:** 10 feet
GPS: 41° 20.737'N, 78° 12.174'W	**Elevation difference:** 1,041 feet
Faces: 279°	**Height:** 1,935 feet
Best times: mid to late afternoon	**Time:** 2 hours
Difficulty: moderate	**Elevation change:** 350 feet
Distance: 4.6 miles	**Best lenses:** 35mm to 100mm

Directions: From the intersection of PA 120 and PA 555 in the town of Driftwood, take PA 555 west through and out of town toward Benezette. As you cross the one-lane bridge, set your odometer. Drive just .7 mile, and turn right onto Mason Hill/Castle Garden Road. In 4 miles, you come to a wide spot on the right adjacent to a deer exclosure gate, with a large wooden sign on the left for the Fred Woods Trail. Park on the right side of the road. GPS coordinates: 41° 21.886'N, 78° 11.018'W

This 4.6-mile loop trail is named for forester Fred Woods, who was fatally injured while on duty. Built by the Young Adult Conservation Corps (YACC) in 1980–81, the trail takes you through some of Woods's favorite terrain. Enjoy. If you have youngsters that are up for a two-hour woodland hike, this is the trail for them. Even it you don't make it past the first viewpoint, a rock garden maze will surely keep any climbing or scrambling child amused for a while.

Cross the road and walk to the right of the sign, and start following the orange blazes. The trail begins as a woods road, so you can move at a fast pace. You cross another woods road in just .14 mile. From here, the Fred Woods Trail narrows to become a true trail. After a pleasant .76-mile stroll, you reach a Y trail divide. This is the head of the 3.05-mile loop to the three views. Turn right along the well-blazed trail where all turns are marked by double blazes. In a few yards, you cross another woods road. In short order, you begin winding around and over boulders that increase in size as you go. At 1.4 miles, a left turn brings you in line with a house-size boulder that looms through the woods.

As you pass between two massive stone blocks at 1.6 miles, you've arrived at the Rock Loop, which is blazed best from the first view back to this point. If you'd like to climb around or turn the kids loose to play, have fun. Continuing along the rock-jumbled trail, you arrive at a medium-size upended boulder at 1.8 miles. This is the first vista.

Though only a narrow alley through the trees, it has its rewards. Looking down this steep-sided view of Sinnemahoning Creek, where Water Plug Hollow dumps in, provides a grand view. Having shot sunrise at the nearby Rocky Mountain Elk Foundation property (Hike 36), I figured this would be a nice nice postdawn stroll to shoot fog-filled valleys. The only problem was that the fog was level with my feet, making shooting impossible. But the thick fog created a relief map for the valley, and it was quite interesting to see how many side drainages the Sinnemahoning has.

After playing around some, return to the main trail and turn right (south) to continue the loop. The trail away from the view will bring you in a few yards to a sign for the Rock Loop, which is to the left. Turn right here. As you pass through some boulders at 2.10 miles, you'll come to a well-beaten but unmarked footpath that bears left. Follow the orange blazes and dead-end at a huge boulder at 2.16 miles. This is the second vista. As you get close to the view, you'll see another trail to the left and perhaps a signpost being held up by a large mountain laurel bush. This is the loop trail's continuation.

As safely as you can, scramble up to the boulder's peak. Here you look a little more south and can see Sinnemahoning Creek meandering around sandbars as it flows toward Driftwood. I like this view because it has so many possibilities, even though you can barely fit a tripod atop the boulder. A little lone scrubby pine sits in the view's center. It's a pleasant-looking tree and shouldn't be a concern.

Climb down from your perch, which is always harder than going up, and turn right to continue your hike. Around 2.4 miles, the trail enters an open woodland and hugs the ridge edge, providing broken views to the right. With the leaves off, this is a beautiful section of trail. As you move along, the trail begins to sweep left at 2.7 miles, where a large opening appears. This is the third vista, and it is a handsome one. When I was here, fog wafted through the trees 50 feet below, creating an ethereal look to the forest. Veeries called back and forth, and the early morning was vibrant with sound. But sadly, the fog eliminated my chances of getting a shot of the Miller Run drainage. Worse, the blueberries I was sitting among weren't ripe yet, so I had to be content with a granola bar. Oh, the trials and tribulations of a nature photographer!

The trail flirts with the ridge edge until slowly leaving it behind at 3.5 miles. Some large rocks slow progress, but they aren't a problem unless you're taking a trail run. Rejoin the loop head at 3.84 miles, turn right, and head back to your car.

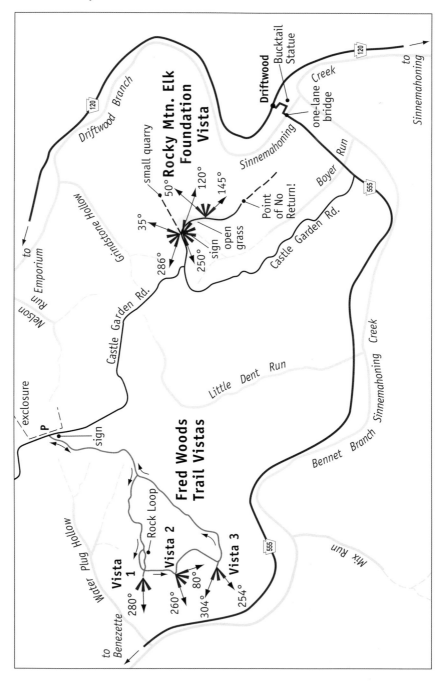

Hike 36	**Rocky Mountain Elk Foundation, Boyer Run, Elk State Forest**

Vista 1

GPS: 41° 20.982′N, 78° 9.194′W	**Field of view:** 246° to 35° and 120° to 250°
Faces: 320° to 185°	

Vista 2

GPS: 41° 20.843′N, 78° 9.071′W	**Field of view:** 50° to 145°
Faces: 100°	
Type: ridge	**Best times:** sunrise through sunset
Rating: 4	**Trail:** none
Relief: 5 feet	**Elevation change:** none
Elevation difference: 1,280 feet	**Best lenses:** 20mm to 400mm
Height: 2,092 feet	

Directions: From the intersection of PA 120 and PA 555 in the town of Driftwood, take PA 555 west through and out of town toward Benezette. As you cross the one-lane bridge, set your odometer. Drive just .7 mile, and turn right onto Mason Hill/Castle Garden Road. Climb the steep road and make the first right at .9 mile. After ascending a short distance, you break out of the trees into a large meadow. Park near the Rocky Mountain Elk Foundation sign. The second view is visible down the spine of the ridge to the southeast.

This 367-acre clear-cut atop Mason Hill is the only location in Elk State Forest with a panoramic view. You can walk as little or as much as you'd like to find a good setup. But before you do, take time get your bearings. This description uses the large sign on the south side of the road as a reference point. From this first vista, you're looking south into the narrow valley created by Sinnemahoning Creek. Toward the left, you can see the road as it follows the terminal spine of Mason Hill. Look right and you can see the deep valley of Mix Run.

Turn your back to the sign and walk across the road to look north up the Driftwood Branch of Sinnemahoning Creek. The northern exposure view isn't as dramatic as the south view, and the ridge drop-off is not as pronounced as on the south side. If you do a quick scan, you'll see a number of lone, scraggly looking trees left from the clear-cutting. You'll have to keep them from view in any shot you try.

By now you'll agree that the south exposure is the better of the two, and if you walk from the sign due south for a few yards, the amount of relief increases. The ridge slope will hide the clear-cut edge for quite a ways, but when it finally comes into view, it just looks nasty. If you go to the edge and stand on an overgrown berm created when the slash was bulldozed, you can

1,000 Feet of Fog. Heavy fog fills the Sinnemahoning Creek and its side drainages almost every morning in summer. You have to take what you can get. *Canon EOS Digital Rebel, Tokina 20–35, polarizer, 2-stop graduate, ISO100 setting, f/8 @ .4 sec.*

get some nice foreground trees. The best shots here are when you get low and fill the foreground with whatever wildflowers you can find.

If you drive down to the next viewpoint, you'll begin to see that the west exposure isn't as good as it looked from higher up. A wide spot provides a convenient place to park, and the best view is left of center looking up Johnson Run. To get some added elevation, stand on your car's roof.

Warning: The road to Vista 2 continues farther down, but there is no other view, even though it looks as if there is. Don't go any farther! Two roads descend from the ridge's south side, and this is one of them. Don't even attempt going down unless you have a bulldozer or other tracked vehicle, because that's what they're meant for. I took my Explorer farther than I should have and was lucky my four-wheel got me back up the hill. Don't say I didn't warn you.

Hike 37 Ives Farm, Grove Hill, Elk State Forest

Type: ridge	**Height:** 2,289 feet
Rating: 3	**Best times:** midmorning to late afternoon
GPS: 41° 24.625'N, 78° 7.025'W	**Difficulty:** easy
Faces: 160°	**Distance:** 1.2 miles
Field of view: 95° to 220°	**Time:** 1 hour
Relief: 5 feet	**Elevation change:** 90 feet
Elevation difference: 100 feet	**Best lenses:** 20mm to 100mm

Directions: From the intersection of PA 120 and PA 872 in Sinnemahoning, take PA 872 north toward Sinnemahoning State Park. In 8.5 miles, turn left onto Brooks Run Road, just after the park entrance on the right and a gas station on the left. Proceed 5.2 miles to a T intersection at Ridge Road, and turn left. Park in .8 mile near a yellow gated forest road on the right. (Turning right onto Ridge will take you to several drivable views, the best of which are the last two, Whitehead Run and Logue Run, located 3.6 miles and 4.3 miles from the turn.) GPS coordinates: 41° 24.619'N, 78° 6.461'W

This is a quick family hike using a forest road that brings you to a unique kind of view—a huge blueberry patch. Begin by walking around the gate and cross a pipeline in .1 mile. A deer exclosure is on the right, labeled Grove Hill #1. Looking carefully, you'll note the difference in forest growth patterns. Within the exclosure is a riot of understory growth, but outside there is none. This is because deer are eating the sapling growth that regenerates the forest, so what is left is heath family plants such as laurel and blueberry that deer won't eat. Extensive ground cover of fern, laurel, and rhododendron are indications of unhealthy forest conditions.

As the road opens up on the left, you'll begin to see a huge blueberry field. Looking along the road's curve, you'll note a hump—that's your destination. Continue to follow the curving road through a gentle climb. Another exclosure appears on the right—this is the old Ives Farm. At the exclosure's end, look for a large open area used as a vehicle turnaround—this is your spot. The road climbs to the right and continues to follow the exclosure fence— this is the Bucktail Path. Another road passes through open heath meadows into a food plot meadow .25 mile farther on. This might be a good location to spot elk before they move down into the Benezette area during the rut. Other wide trails braid the area near the exclosure, so feel free to explore.

With your back to the exclosure, the view is of the undulating terrain of Grove Hill. On the right, you can make out the end of Big Run drainage, which appears as a long depression. Along the axis of view, the terrain falls away gently all the way to Sinnemahoning Creek, so the ridges you see in the distance are on the far side of Stevenson Dam at Sinnemahoning State Park.

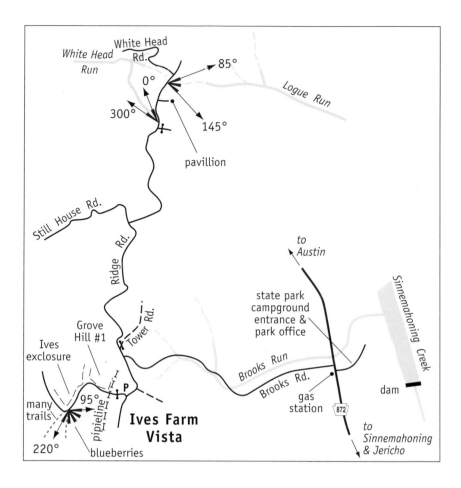

On my way in, I saw several elk tracks, one set of which indicated a cow and calf pair. I wandered around looking for additional sign but could only find spore piles in the food plot meadow. Although not a spectacular cliff or ledge view, the Ives Farm provides a large number of splendid photographic opportunities. Even though shooting conditions were less than ideal, I spent more than an hour just wandering around soaking in the solitude of the location.

Hike 38 Whittimore Tower, Elk State Forest

Type: ridge	Height: 2,233 feet
Rating: 3	Best times: midafternoon through sunset
GPS: 41° 28.869'N, 78° 15.922'W	Difficulty: moderate
Faces: west view 270°, south view 157°	Distance: 2 miles
Fields of view: vistos	Time: 1 hour
Relief: 5 feet	Elevation change: 370 feet
Elevation difference: 600 feet	Best lenses: 20mm to 100mm

Directions: From the intersection of PA 120 and PA 155 on the east end of Emporium, take PA 120 west into town for 1 mile, and turn left at the traffic light onto Broad Street. As soon as you cross the creek, the road becomes Whittimore Road. Follow uphill for 3.4 miles to the intersection with May Hollow Road (T 312), and turn right to continue on Whittimore. Proceed for 1.1 miles, and make a hard left onto a gated forest road. Park near the gate but not blocking it. GPS coordinates: 41° 28.731'N, 78° 15.922'W

This road hike takes you to a rare kind of vista—a fire tower with a view. Most fire towers are fenced off and closed, and if they are accessible, it's only because the fences have fallen down. In general, climbing any closed tower is dangerous because of damage from rust and decay. It's rare that fire tower sites have views, since the towers are meant to reach above the trees, but Whittimore Tower sits on a small knob atop Whittimore Hill, and the surrounding terrain has been cleared and seeded for wildlife, providing two openings. From the parking spot, walk around the gate and uphill 1 mile to the tower. Set up near the western corner of the tower's fence. Both view directions can be worked from one position.

The west view is purely a long-lens shot looking in the general direction of St. Mary's. The plateau falls off in this direction, so the view is long though narrow. The west view is a visto type, and it's best to come here when the evening sky has chance of looking good enough to shoot the clouds.

The south view looks out over the headwaters region of Sterling Run drainage. It's also a long-lens shot, but you can work a wide-angle if you take the time to check your frame edges. This is an anytime-of-day shot and looks best when light fog fills the valleys below.

If you'd like another nice view that's drivable, Salt Run Vista is not too far out of the way. From Emporium, follow PA 155 north to Sizerville State Park. Turn right onto Crooked Run Road just as you enter the park; then bear right onto Ridge Road. The view is .3 mile along Ridge Road on the right side. If you hit Portage Road, you went too far.

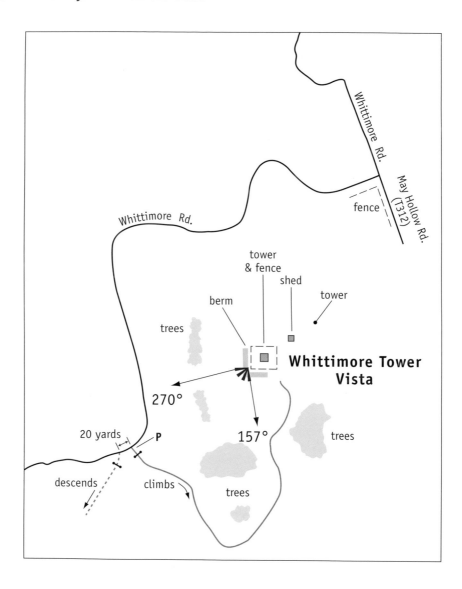

| Hike 39 | **Fish Dam Wild Area, Sproul State Forest** |

Type: ridge	**Elevation difference:** 1,080 feet
Rating: 4	**Height:** 2,198 feet
GPS: 41° 14.169'N, 77° 46.980'W	**Best times:** midafternoon through sunset
Faces: 300°	**Trail:** none
Field of view: 210° to 340°	**Elevation change:** none
Relief: 20 feet	**Best lenses:** 20mm to 100mm

Directions: From the intersection of PA 120 and PA 144 in Renovo, take PA 144 south for 10 miles to a large parking area and viewing platform on the right.

As tourism has increased, the Department of Conservation and Natural Resources (DCNR) has begun to cater more to the nonhiker, and this viewing platform is a superb addition to that effort. Looking out over Fish Dam Wild Area, this vista provides an outstanding view of the Allegheny Plateau's extensive creek drainage network. To the left are Fish Dam Run and Proctor Hollow; in the center is the Dennison Fork; and on the extreme right, hidden by trees, is an unnamed drainage sitting below a divide created by Barney's Ridge. Everything in front of you drains into the Susquehanna's West Branch.

This is an outstanding sunset location, where you can work wide and long lenses with abandon. The best setup is on the upper platform near the Who Lives in the Big Woods sign.

As I waited out an approaching thunderstorm, I decided to sit quietly against a fence post. Birds that had rushed for cover when I arrived slowly returned. Three male ruby-crowned kinglets landed on branches a dozen feet away, and soon a pair of male goldfinches arrived. While

Daisies. Great foregrounds can come in small packages, so take care to look for them. In this case, a small bunch of daisies, no bigger than a shoebox, makes this image. *Canon EOS Digital Rebel, Tokina 20–35, polarizer, 2-stop graduate, ISO100 setting, f/8 @ .3 sec.*

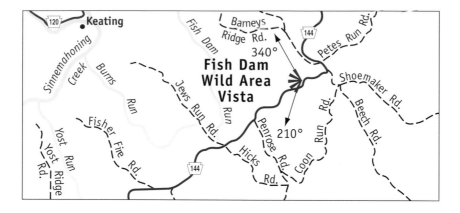

the kinglets sat quietly, the finches proceeded to do battle in a fluttering yellow blur. A light shower began, punctuated by a low, throaty boom of thunder, yet I remained still to see what would happen next. As the finches flitted after each other, the kinglets skittered from branch to branch like kids playing tag. In a few minutes, they came within 5 feet of me before settling down. If only I had a long lens setup! It just goes to show what can happen when you make an effort to become part of the landscape.

The Sproul State Forest Map notes two other nearby views to the north, one along the Chuck Keiper Trail about .25 mile north and the other along Barney's Ridge Road about 1 mile north. Both are long since overgrown and not worth your effort. Two others to the east, one at Pete's Run and the other in Cranberry Swamp Natural Area, are also overgrown. Several other signed views lie along PA 144 southbound toward Snow Shoe. Though they didn't make this guide on their own merits, you may want to take the time to check them out anyway.

Hike 40 Hyner View State Park, Sproul State Forest

Type: ledge	**Elevation difference:** 1,260 feet
Rating: 5+	**Height:** 1,940 feet
GPS: 41° 19.574'N, 77° 37.486'W	**Best times:** any time is good, but best at sunset
Faces: 255°	**Trail:** none
Field of view: 150° to 360°	**Elevation change:** none
Relief: 100 feet	**Best lenses:** 20mm to 400mm

Directions: From the intersection of PA 120 and PA 144 in Renovo, take PA 120 east 6.5 miles. Turn left onto Hyner Run Road, following signs for Hyner Run and Hyner View State Parks. In 1.8 miles, make a hard right to climb to Hyner View. Follow the narrow, twisting, paved park road to the view.

Sunset at Hyner View. Sunset was looking like a bust until I noticed a small stand of flea-bane near the hang glider launch platform below the view. Using it as an anchoring fore-ground made all the difference. *Tachihara 4x5 field camera, 150mm Schneider Symmar f/5.6, polarizer, 2-stop graduate, 81A warming filter, 6x7 roll film back, Kodak E100VS, f/32 @ 10 sec.*

This is arguably the best drivable view in all of Penn's Woods. Nowhere else in the state can you get a view like this. Sitting atop the viewpoint's wall looking west, I watched a thunderstorm move up the valley. Although I couldn't as yet hear thunder, the quality of the clouds, the thickness of the air, and the fact that the Susquehanna River was slowly disappearing behind a gray veil of rain didn't bode well for my prospects of getting a good shot.

When I finally saw a flash of lightning, I walked back to my car and rode out a violent but brief squall. As the storm cleared and the sun dipped

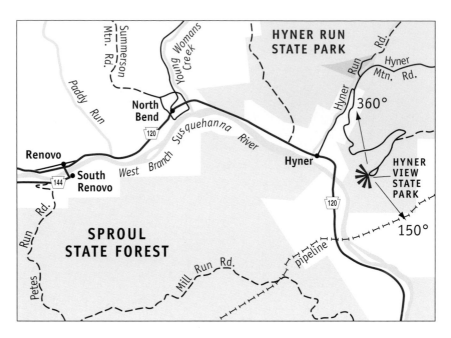

below the clouds, I knew my chance had come. This truly is an amazing location. Even though I got some nice shots, I had missed an incredible event the previous week—a mass hang glider fly-off. Before you visit, contact Hyner View State Park to find out when this summer event will happen, and get here early to shoot a unique spectacle.

Hike 41 Ramm Road, Mid State Trail, Tiadaghton State Forest

Type: ridge	**Elevation difference:** 1,064 feet
Rating: 4+	**Height:** 1,817 feet
GPS: 41° 7.703'N, 77° 17.340'W	**Best times:** sunrise to late afternoon
Faces: 90°	**Trail:** none
Field of view: 60° to 120°	**Elevation change:** none
Relief: 5 feet	**Best lenses:** 50mm to 400mm

Directions: The orange-blazed Mid State Trail spends about 1 mile on Ramm Road, which is itself a drivable trail. This view of Nippenose Valley is incredible, so whether you walk or drive, make sure you're here for sunrise. To get there from I-80, get off at Exit 192 and follow signs for PA 880 and Carrol. In Carrol, turn onto PA 880 east toward Rauchtown for 6.7 miles. Turn left onto Pine Mountain Road and follow for 3.6 miles. Where it crests a steep ridge, make a hard left onto Ramm Road. Climb the rough woods road, and you will arrive at the view in 1.5 miles.

The view through a wide tree gap looks out on the picturesque Nippenose Valley, filled with the same fine-looking farms you drove past while on Pine Mountain Road. With around 1,000 feet of elevation differential, you feel like you're flying. Wide-angles work well here because surrounding trees are healthy and provide a nice frame to the scene. This is one of the few locations where I wouldn't use a graduated filter to even out exposures for the foreground. Only worry about the valley being properly exposed with respect to the sky, and let the foreground go dark. This will create a nice frame to the scene. To gain a little elevation, park right at the view and stand on the roof of your vehicle.

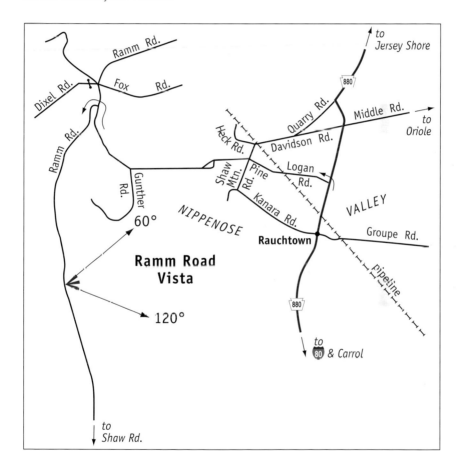

Nippenose Valley. Climbing on my truck roof provides just enough relief to reveal a spectacular view of Nippenose Valley. *Canon EOS Digital Rebel, Tokina 20–35, polarizer, ISO100 setting, f/8 @ 1/60 sec.*

Hike 42 Ramsey Road Overlook, Tiadaghton State Forest

Type: ledge	**Elevation difference:** 1,198 feet
Rating: 4	**Height:** 1,805 feet
GPS: 41° 18.286'N, 77° 20.588'W	**Best times:** midafternoon through sunset
Faces: 240°	**Trail:** none
Field of view: 170° to 312°	**Elevation change:** none
Relief: 15 feet	**Best lenses:** 20mm to 100mm

Directions: From the entrance of Little Pine State Park, take the camping-area access road for .3 mile to where it joins English Run Road adjacent to the dam. Follow English Run for 3.6 miles, merging with Limbaugh Road. Stay on Limbaugh for 4.4 miles, until the Y intersection at Parker Road. Turn left, staying with Limbaugh for .8 mile. Pass Dam Run Road; then turn right onto Ramsey/Moore Road at a hunting camp. In .2 mile, bear right onto Ramsey and proceed for 3 miles to a parking spot on the right.

The ledges here are 50 feet across, with several nice perches to work from. The view left provides a classic view of nested ridges, and in the morning you can get Pine Creek's west side in rim light. Facing right toward Waterville, which is hidden from view, PA 44 appears as a bright line during the mid-day or in late afternoon. Work this location when the east side of Pine Creek is in shadow.

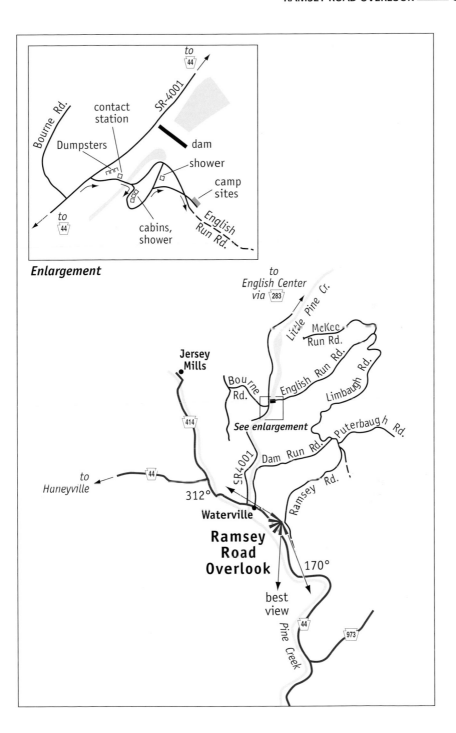

Enlargement

Pine Creek Panorama. Shooting panoramas is fun, with the right software. Remove the polarizer, and set and fix the exposure. Then overlap about 20 percent between frames, keeping the horizon in the middle. I used a stitch utility that came with my Canon Digital Rebel and cropped out the blank sky. After I was done, I used Adobe Photoshop to correct any minor exposure differences between frames. *Canon EOS Digital Rebel, Tokina 20–35, polarizer, ISO100 setting, f/16 @ ¹/30 sec.*

Hike 43 Sinking Spring Overlook, Tiadaghton State Forest

Type: ridge	**Elevation difference:** 1,321 feet
Rating: 4	**Height:** 1,987 feet
GPS: 41° 21.420'N, 77° 25.708'W	**Best times:** midmorning through late afternoon
Faces: 10°	**Trail:** none
Field of view: 340° to 40°	**Elevation change:** none
Relief: 10 feet	**Best lenses:** 20mm to 300mm

Directions: From the intersection of PA 44 and PA 664 in Haneyville, take PA 44 north for .8 mile. Turn right onto Browns Run/Zinc Fork Road, then bear left to stay on Browns Run Road. In 1.5 miles, turn right onto Sinking Spring Road. After 2 miles, turn left onto the unsigned Sinking Spring Spur Road, following it to the dead-end overlook.

Sinking Spring Road is one of the best gravel forest roads in the state. Sinking Spring Spur is not, so take it slow. This dead-end road brings you to a fine view of Pine Creek north of Waterville. If foreground growth is an issue, park near the extent of the view area and climb on your car's roof. The foreground relief is McClure Run, and the two humps beyond are ridges separating Shanty Run and Solomon Run, which is near a road at Blue Stone.

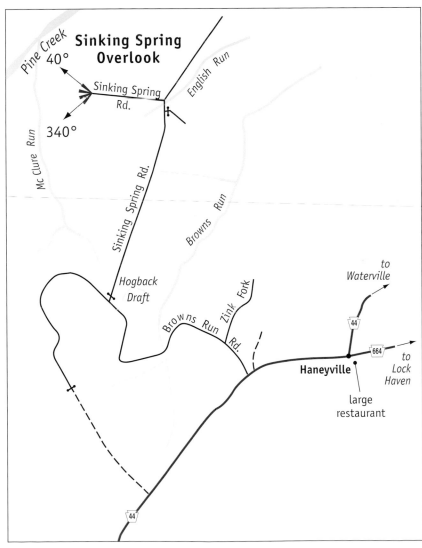

Pine Creek

40°

Sinking Spring Overlook

English Run

Sinking Spring Rd.

340°

Mc Clure Run

Sinking Spring Rd.

Browns Run

Hogback Draft

Zink Fork

to Waterville

Browns Run Rd.

44

664

Haneyville

to Lock Haven

large restaurant

44

Hike 44 Black Forest Trail, Tiadaghton State Forest

Grade Trail Vista

Type: ridge	Field of view: visto
Rating: 2	Relief: 5 feet
GPS: 41° 27.830'N, 77° 34.104'W	Elevation difference: 386 feet
Faces: 90°	Height: 2,122 feet

White Birch Lookout

Type: ridge	Field of view: 320° to 250°
Rating: 4	Relief: 10 feet
GPS: 41° 28.314'N, 77° 32.700'W	Elevation difference: 725 feet
Faces: 350°	Height: 2,141 feet

Moss Hollow Lookout

Type: ridge	Field of view: 125° to 190°
Rating: 4	Relief: 10 feet
GPS: 41° 28.314'N, 77° 32.532'W	Elevation difference: 1,025 feet
Faces: 160°	Height: 2,114 feet

Canyon Vista

Type: ridge	Field of view: 92° to 176°
Rating: 5	Relief: 10 feet
GPS: 41° 28.232'N, 77° 31.955'W	Elevation difference: 1,321 feet
Faces: 134°	Height: 2,056 feet
Best times: early morning	Trail: Black Forest Trail
Trail: Grade trail	Difficulty: easy to moderate
Difficulty: easy	Distance: 4.7 miles
Distance: .9 mile	Time: 2 hours
Time: 30 minutes	Elevation change: Black Forest Trail 190 feet
Elevation change: Grade Trail 50 feet	Best lenses: 35mm to 125mm

Directions: From the intersection of PA 44 and PA 414 north of Jersey Shore, take PA 44 north for 5.3 miles to where it joins PA 664 in Haneyville. Turn right to continue on PA 44 for 13 miles to Manor Fork Road, where you turn right into a forest maintenance facility and park behind it. Manor Fork is marked by several white clapboard buildings and a colonnade of big pines. The maintenance facility appears as a red dot on the Tioga State Forest Map just north of "Pump Station." The three PA 44 vistas noted on the state forest map are overgrown. GPS coordinates: 41° 28.100'N, 77° 33.975'W

Moss Hollow. This was simply a glorious day to go for a walk. *Tachihara 4x5 field camera, 90mm Schneider Angulaon-S f/6.8, polarizer, 1-stop graduate, 4x5 Ready Load holder, Kodak E100VS, f/16 @ 1/8 sec.*

After several brutally hot days capped off by violent nightly thunder storms, I was more than ready for some good hiking weather, and the afternoon I did this section of the Black Forest Trail was simply a perfect day. From the parking area behind the maintenance shed, walk up Manor Road a few yards. Ahead is the gated road of the Gas Line Trail, and to the right is the wide, ungated woods road of the Grade Trail.

Turn right onto the signed, blue-blazed Grade Trail. This old rail grade is wide and level, and it makes for a quick bit of hiking. At .15 mile, look for a large opening on the left where another trail drops away. A sign facing away from you marks the left turn onto the Naval Run Trail, which descends all the way to Pine Creek. Turn left and walk down a couple yards into a large blueberry patch. This huge opening is the Grade Trail Vista. Where you stand will determine the direction and field of view. I decided to hang out close to the Grade Trail. The view is OK, but what I really enjoyed was the ability to eat and shoot. After you've had your fill of film or blueberries, return to Manor Road.

The mileages begin again here from Manor Road. Walk around the gate onto the blue-blazed Gas Line Trail. The road follows a pole line for a short distance but bears left away from it at .13 mile. Although this road trail is boring, it's humanely level, and you can set a brisk pace. At 1.15 miles, the red-blazed Black Forest Trail (BFT) joins from the left. Continue straight along the woods road. A signed side trail for White Birch Lookout appears on the left at 1.28 miles. Turn left and walk the short distance to the view.

This wonderful classic Pennsylvania mountain view consists of an open area among pines framed by two mature white birches. Facing north, over-looking the headwaters of Little Slate Run, the view is long and grand. A small bench completes the scene. As I sat here jotting notes in my field journal, gentle breezes wafted through the pines, announcing themselves with soft sounds long before they could be felt. This whispering purr of wind through long-needled pines is the delicate call of Penn's Woods, which can work magic on the tired soul.

Returning to the BFT, turn left, and in a short distance you'll come to another sign. Turn right here for Moss Hollow Lookout. From the short side

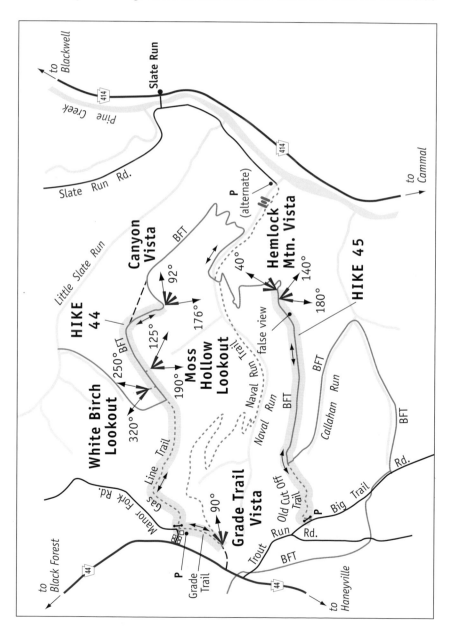

trail, you get a good look at the view before it really opens up. Gazing down on Naval Run, you can make out where it joins Pine Creek on the left. Directly across the valley is a sharp-topped ridge covered in hemlocks. This is Hemlock Mountain, which should be your next hike (Hike #45). The only thing marring the view is a power-line cut 6.7 miles away.

Return again to the BFT, and turn right to continue along the level road grade. At 2 miles, a sign marks a right turn where the BFT bears away from the road. Now on a trail, you make a meandering shallow descent through open woods, arriving at Canyon Vista at 2.35 miles. Another bench conveniently placed against a curved tree trunk invites you to sit for a while to soak up the view. The power line seen from Moss Hollow Lookout is not visible from this position, but two small clear-cuts on the opposite ridge will be an issue in bright midday sun. I'm concerned that these cuts, which are on private land above the village of Slate Run, are not logging activity, but building-lot cutouts. If that's the case, the sumptuous view will be forever scarred.

To return to your car, reverse your route. You'll arrive at the gate fronting Manor Road at 4.7 miles.

Hike 45 | Hemlock Mountain, Black Forest Trail, Tiadaghton State Forest

Vista 1

Type: ridge	**Field of view:** visto
Rating: 5	**Relief:** 5 feet
GPS: 41° 27.460'N, 77° 31.897'W	**Elevation difference:** 1,087 feet
Faces: 148°	**Height:** 2,097 feet

Vista 2

Type: ridge	**Field of view:** 140° to 180°
Rating: 2	**Relief:** 5 feet
GPS: 41° 27.463'N, 77° 31.794'W	**Elevation difference:** 1,353 feet
Faces: 40°	**Height:** 2,058 feet
Best times: late morning through late afternoon	**Time:** 2 hours
Difficulty: moderate	**Elevation change:** 390 feet
Distance: 4 miles	**Best lenses:** 20mm to 300mm

Directions: From the intersection of PA 44 and PA 414 north of Jersey Shore, take PA 44 north for 5.3 miles to where it joins PA 664 in Haneyville. Turn right to continue on PA 44 for 12.4 miles to Trout Run Road, where you turn right. In .5 mile, bear left onto Big Trail Road. In .2 mile, park at a wide spot on the left in front of the log-gated Old Cutoff Trail. GPS coordinates: 41° 27.227'N, 77° 33.838'W

The Old Cutoff Trail is wide and obvious, with blue blazes more visible on the return route because they're painted on just one side of the trees. Walk around the gate and begin descending immediately. The trail sweeps left, and as it bottoms out on a wide bench, it turns right at .1 mile. To the left, the ridge drops into Naval Run, and on the right is the rise supporting the road.

After a straight level section, the trail turns left and drops at .35 mile. You'll arrive at a large grassy intersection with the orange-blazed Black Forest Trail (BFT) at .6 mile. Turn left to stay along the ridge's spine. (A right would take you into Callahan Run.) From here the BFT goes over a hump and then continues to descend into a narrow saddle of the dividing ridge separating Naval Run from Callahan Run. You begin a long climb, with one

Earth Shadow. I waited two weeks for a clear day to shoot the earth's shadow at sunset from here. The pale blue layer is earth's own shadow in the atmosphere. The contrast of blue and pink are accentuated by a 10CC magenta filter. Conditions like this are magical and demand that you keep shooting until you can no longer see. *Tachihara 4x5 field camera, 210mm Schneider Symmar-S f/5.6, polarizer, 2-stop graduate, 10CC magenta, 4x5 Ready Load holder, Kodak E100VS, f/32 @ 20 sec.*

steep section lasting about .3 mile. About halfway up the steep part, you enter an old view cutout at 1.53 miles. From here, the pitch slackens. The ascent tops out over a small hump, and the first view is located just beyond 1.95 miles. This is by far the best view of Pine Creek outside of Colton Point State Park and Bradley Wales Picnic Area. Looking down lower Pine Creek, you'll see that the twisting creek provides a wide separation of the surrounding ridges which overlap nicely.

If you stand at the back of the nearby fire ring, you'll note a tree on the right with a burl or exposed knot about two feet above the ground. Look closely and a smirking face will appear in the bark. Once you find it, you won't be able to ignore it because the eyes seem to follow you as you move. A large power line below Cammal is almost hidden by the terrain. Another view looking north is a short way up the BFT, but it's not very good.

The Big Trail Road roadside view below the Stone Quarry Trail noted on the Tiadaghton forest map is overgrown, but a decent view .8 mile down the road looks east down Callahan Run into the gorge.

Hike 46 Ice Break, West Rim Trail, Pine Creek Gorge

Type: ledge	Height: 1,648 feet
Rating: 3	Best times: midmorning through late afternoon
GPS: 41° 39.493'N, 77° 28.320'W	Difficulty: easy; woods road
Faces: 145°	Distance: 1.4 miles
Field of view: 40° to 165°	Time: 1 hour, 30 minutes
Relief: 50 feet	Elevation change: 50 feet
Elevation difference: 644 feet	Best lenses: 80mm to 125mm

Directions: From Wellsboro, take US 6 west for 11.2 miles to Ansonia. Cross Marsh Creek and turn left onto Colton Road. After 4.4 miles, you enter Colton Point State Park, turning right to continue along Colton Road. In 2 miles, make a hard left onto West Rim Road at the Y intersection with Painter Leetonia and Colton Roads. In another 2 miles, make another hard left to continue on West Rim Road at a Y intersection with Thompson Hollow Road. In 5.6 miles, park at wide spot near the marked trailhead for the Ice Break Trail. GPS coordinates: 41° 39.335'N, 77° 28.978'W

From the parking area, walk down the Ice Break Trail, a wide, blue-blazed woods road, until it hits the orange-blazed West Rim Trail. The vista is marked by a fire ring, fence, and red case holding a trail register. From here, the best view is looking downstream, although setting up on the extreme

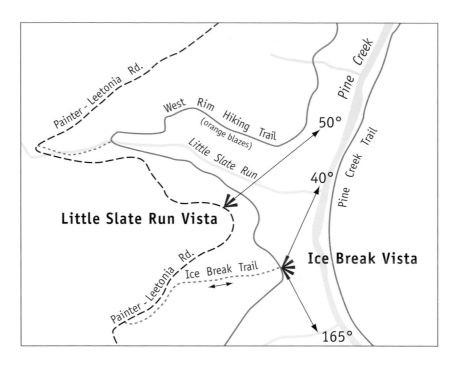

right does provide an adequate view upstream. The left foreground has a number of spindly trees that may become overgrown to the point of fouling the entire view.

Don't bother continuing northbound along the West Rim Trail to the next vista noted on the West Rim Trail map and guide, as it's totally overgrown. A decent roadside view called Little Slate Run Vista, which you passed on the way, sits immediately above Ice Break Vista at 41° 39.718′N, 77° 28.549′W. It provides some fine images of the Slate Run drainage.

Hike 47 **Bradley Wales Picnic Area, Pine Creek Gorge**

Vista 1

Type: cliff	**Field of view:** 340° to 110°
Rating: 4	**Relief:** 200 feet
GPS: 41° 38.711'N, 77° 27.535'W	**Elevation difference:** 550 feet
Faces: 90° and 340°	**Height:** 1,544 feet

Vista 2

Type: cliff	**Field of view:** 348° to 120°
Rating: 5	**Relief:** 200 feet
GPS: 41° 38.766'N, 77° 27.694'W	**Elevation difference:** 644 feet
Faces: 100° and 348°	**Height:** 1,638 feet

Vista 3

Type: cliff	**Field of view:** 350° to 90°
Rating: 3	**Relief:** 200 feet
GPS: 41° 38.640'N, 77° 27.339'W	**Elevation difference:** 599 feet
Faces: 100° and 348°	**Height:** 1,593 feet
Best times: any time	**Time:** 20 minutes
Difficulty: easy	**Elevation change:** 100 feet
Distance: .4 mile	**Best lenses:** 35mm to 75mm

Directions: From Wellsboro, take US 6 west for 11.2 miles to Ansonia. Cross Marsh Creek and turn left onto Colton Road. After 4.4 miles, you enter Colton Point State Park, turning right to continue along Colton Road. In 2 miles, make a hard left onto West Rim Road at a Y intersection with Painter Leetonia and Colton Roads. In another 2 miles, make another hard left to continue on West Rim Road at a Y intersection with Thompson Hollow Road. In 6.4 miles, make yet another left at a Y intersection with Painter Leetonia Road to stay on West Rim Road. In 1 mile, bear left into Bradley Wales. After you pass a pit toilet, the first parking area is on the left where the road makes a sharp right turn at a wide spot. GPS coordinates: 41° 38.693'N, 77° 27.503'W. The second parking area is where the road ends. GPS coordinates: 41° 38.640'N, 77° 27.339'W

It seems as if Bradley Wales has been overlooked for the more popular views at Colton Point and Leonard Harrison State Parks, which is a shame, because this area is a real gem. From the first parking area, there is a fenced view looking north up the creek. Walk past this, heading north, up a wide pine-shrouded trail about 100 yards to the first vista, marked by a long stone and wood fence. Here you'll find two shooting positions, one at the extreme right standing near a stump, and the other at the extreme left between two

Clearing Fog at Pine Creek. Heavy fog shrouded every sunrise vista in Tioga State Forest, so I just wandered around until I found a spot where the fog was beginning to break. It doesn't look like it, but this shot was made almost four hours after sunrise. *Canon EOS Digital Rebel, Tokina 20–35, polarizer, ISO100 setting, f/8 @ ¹/₈₀ sec.*

closely spaced pines. If you look at the opposite rim, you'll see several meadows, one of which has an enormous house in it. Talk about the proverbial million-dollar view!

Continue up the wide trail, climbing as you go, and you'll reach the second vista at .2 mile. As with the other view, the best positions are on the extreme left and right. The best right-hand position is again near a stump, while the best left-hand is on the next-to-last fence post near a tree.

For the third vista, head back to your car, drive to the road's end, and park. Here, a fence wraps around the parking loop. Setting up left of the fence on a ledge doesn't afford the long gorge view you'd expect, but the right side gives a nice look at the deep scars created by Ice Break and Slate Runs.

On the way into Bradley Wales, you passed a poor-looking roadside view at 41° 39.101′N, 77° 28.293′W, about .5 mile before you turned off West Rim Road. Although you may have stopped and given it a quick look, I recommend you go back now for a second one. In my field journal, I rated this view highly for one reason, and it's hanging off the cliffs opposite along a bearing of 30°. To see what I mean, make a steep 100-yard descent into the view cutout to where the slope drops off quickly at some exposed rocks. With a set of binoculars, look across Ice Break Run and slightly below your current elevation. Near the far cliff tops is a lone juniper tree leaning into

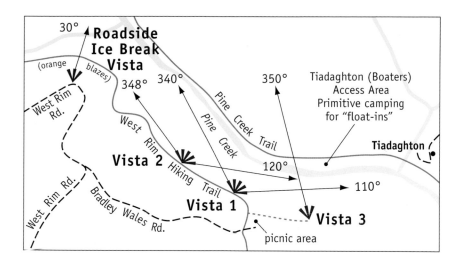

space like a Zen painting. A moderate to long telephoto will provide an excellent image of this gravity-defying shrub. The background is supported by nesting ridges of Ice Break and Slate Runs. In fall, use a wide aperture to create a soft, colorful background. If you can catch this lovely tree with rim lighting at sunrise, you'll have an incredible image.

Hike 48 Cushman Hollow, Tioga State Forest

Type: ridge	**Elevation difference:** 678 feet
Rating: 5	**Height:** 2,230 feet
GPS: 41° 36.258'N, 77° 33.391'W	**Best times:** sunrise through late morning
Faces: 145°	**Trail:** none
Field of view: 88° to 202°	**Elevation change:** none
Relief: 10 feet	**Best lenses:** 17mm to 50mm

Directions: From Wellsboro, take US 6 west for 11.2 miles to Ansonia. Cross Marsh Creek and turn left onto Colton Road. After 4.4 miles, you enter Colton Point State Park, turning right to continue along Colton Road. In 2 miles, make a hard left onto West Rim Road at a Y intersection with Painter Leetonia and Colton Roads. In another 2 miles, make another hard left to continue on West Rim Road at a Y intersection with Thompson Hollow Road. In 6.4 miles, bear right onto Painter Leetonia Road at a Y intersection and follow for 3.9 miles into the old CCC Camp of Leetonia. Turn right onto Cedar Run Road. In .6 mile, turn left onto Buck Run Road. In 3.1 miles, turn left onto Buck Ridge Road just after crossing a pipeline cut. At a T intersection where Buck Ridge turns right, proceed straight on Cushman Road for .4 mile to a large cutout on the left.

The broad, rolling hills of Cushman Hollow Vista should not be missed. This is an incredible view. From the vista sitting at 2,230 feet in elevation, the view stretches forever, looking down Cushman Run on the left and a number of hollows that gather together on the right, forming Frying Pan and Buck Runs and Slide Island Draft near Leetonia. Along 186°, you can see an open area that was the CCC Camp at Leetonia. If you're lucky enough to have good clouds at dawn, tilt up for a vaulting cloudscape.

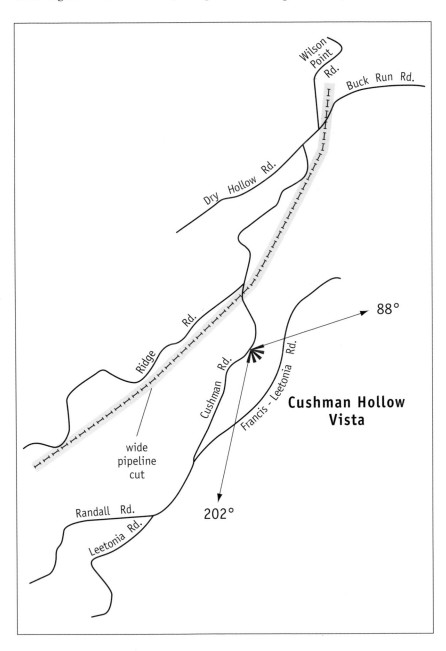

Cotton Candy Dawn. Skies like this happen only a few times a year. When you're in the right place at the right time, it's pure magic. Just don't forget to take time to enjoy the moment. *Canon EOS Digital Rebel, Tokina 20–35, 10CC magenta, ISO100 setting, f/16 @ 1.6 sec.*

Hike 49   Elk Run, Tioga State Forest

Type: ridge	**Elevation difference:** 644 feet
Rating: 4	**Height:** 1,648 feet
GPS: 41° 39.408'N, 77° 31.882'W	**Best times:** midmorning through late afternoon
Faces: 000°	**Trail:** none
Field of view: 330° to 32°	**Elevation change:** none
Relief: 20 feet	**Best lenses:** 17mm to 100mm

Directions: From Wellsboro, take US 6 west for 11.2 miles to Ansonia. Cross Marsh Creek and turn left onto Colton Road. After 4.4 miles, you enter Colton Point State Park, turning right to continue along Colton Road. In 2 miles, make a hard left onto West Rim Road at a Y intersection with Painter Leetonia and Colton Roads. In another 2 miles, bear right at a Y intersection onto Thompson Hollow Road. In 2.6 miles, at a T intersection of Thompson Hollow and Mill Run Roads, turn left to stay on Thompson Hollow. In 1 mile, turn left onto Cedar Mountain/Elk Run Road. In 1.3 miles, bear right at a Y where Mill Run Road rejoins to stay on Cedar Mountain/Elk Run Road. The road makes two looping turns around creek sheds, arriving at the road cutout at 1.8 miles.

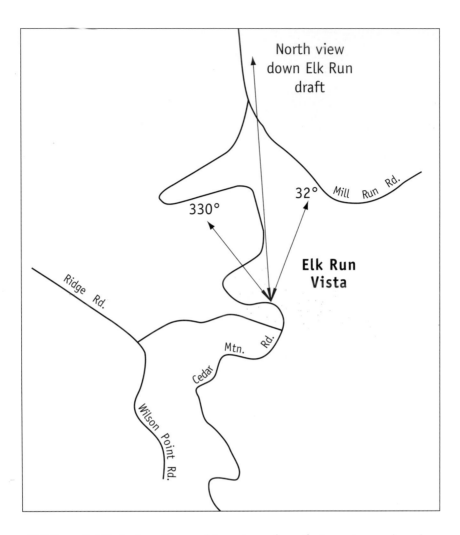

North view
down Elk Run
draft

32° Mill Run Rd.

330°

**Elk Run
Vista**

Ridge Rd.

Mtn. Rd.

Cedar

Wilson Point Rd.

Sitting slightly below the road is a steep drop that creates a nice view looking up the headwater drainages that eventually form Elk Run. Although the view is primarily of Elk Run, you can make out the upper reaches of Cedar and Little Slate Run as well. This is a great fall foliage spot. Another view just .5 mile south is mostly overgrown and not worth the time.

Hike 50	**Colton Point State Park, Pine Creek Gorge**

View 1

Type: cliff	Field of view: 60° to 175°
Rating: 5	Relief: 250 feet
GPS: 41° 42.498′N, 77° 27.941′W	Elevation difference: 593 feet
Faces: 65° and 170°	Height: 1,675 feet

Pavilion 1

Type: cliff	Field of view: visto
Rating: 3	Relief: 200 feet
GPS: 41° 42.310′N, 77° 27.956′W	Elevation difference: 567 feet
Faces: 60°	Height: 1,649 feet

Pavilion 3

Type: cliff	Field of view: visto
Rating: 5	Relief: 200 feet
GPS: 41° 42.149′N, 77° 27.910′W	Elevation difference: 584 feet
Faces: 45°	Height: 1,673 feet

Pavilion 5A

Type: cliff	Field of view: visto
Rating: 2	Relief: 200 feet
GPS: 41° 42.046′N, 77° 27.848′W	Elevation difference: 503 feet
Faces: 34° and 80°	Height: 1,592 feet

Pavilion 5B

Type: ledge	Field of view: 30° to 150°
Rating: 4	Relief: 120 feet
GPS: 41° 42.006′N, 77° 27.812′W	Elevation difference: 421 feet
Faces: 90°	Height: 1,510 feet
Best times: any time	Time: 30 minutes
Difficulty: easy	Elevation change: 270 feet
Distance: .8 mile	Best lenses: 50mm to 125mm

Directions: From Wellsboro, take US 6 west for 11.2 miles to Ansonia. Cross Marsh Creek and turn left onto Colton Road. Follow for 4.3 miles to a large parking area on the right with a large sign and a viewpoint on the left. To get to the second parking area, continue along Colton Road for .1 mile, passing Deadman Hollow Road. Make a hard left off of Colton Road and park in a small lot between Pavilions 1 and 2. GPS coordinates for the second parking area: 41° 42.326′N, 77° 28.004′W

Colton Point State Park has five nice viewpoints that you can either walk or drive to. The best views are the first one upon entering the park and the one near pavilion 3.

Begin from the first parking area you come to, walking across the road and descending a short flight of stairs to the large viewing platform. This 250-foot cliff is the most popular location in the park, so parking will be at premium during peak fall color. The view looks both upstream and down and provides a number of great setups, with the best position being on the platform's left side near a large tree.

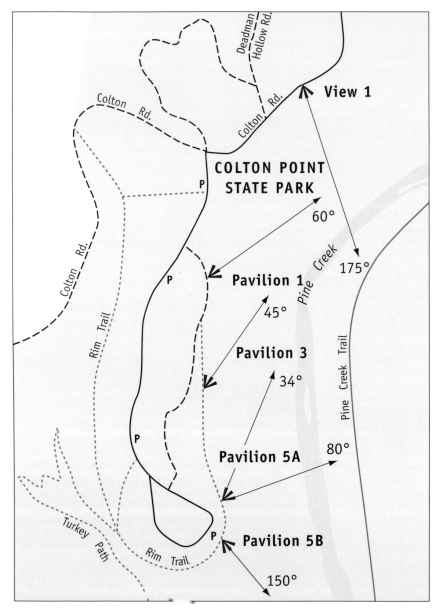

Move on to the second parking area between Pavilions 1 and 2, and walk downhill past Pavilion 1 to a fenced so-so northeast exposure hemmed in by large pines. Turn right and walk down the gravel one-way road, passing Pavilion 2 and bearing left off the road to follow the blue-blazed Rim Trail. Just beyond Pavilion 3 at .23 mile is a tree-covered vista with a great northeast exposure. Continuing along, after a shallow descent, you reach another vista close to the paved loop at Pavilion 5, followed quickly by the last view, adjacent to the loop parking area. This last view is wheelchair-accessible with some assistance. Although it sits at the end of Colton Point, the view from here is only of the east rim, so it's not much of a view. To return to your car, reverse your route or walk along the gravel road back to the parking area.

Hike 51 Barbour Rock, West Rim Trail, Mileposts 3 to 4, Pine Creek Gorge

Barbour Rock

Type: cliff	**Field of view:** 130° to 250°
Rating: 4	**Relief:** 300 feet
GPS: 41° 43.127′N, 77° 27.070′W	**Elevation difference:** 761 feet
Faces: 230°	**Height:** 1,870 feet

Vista 2

Type: cliff	**Field of view:** 122° to 290°
Rating: 5	**Relief:** 70 feet
GPS: 41° 43.118′N, 77° 27.109′W	**Elevation difference:** 715 feet
Faces: 212°	**Height:** 1,824 feet

Vista 3

Type: ledge	**Field of view:** 190° to 210°
Rating: 4	**Relief:** 20 feet
GPS: 41° 43.090′N, 77° 27.423′W	**Elevation difference:** 722 feet
Faces: 200°	**Height:** 1,831 feet
Best times: any time	**Trail:** Road Loop
Trail: Barbour Rock Loop	**Difficulty:** easy
Difficulty: easy	**Distance:** 2.6 miles
Distance: 1.1 miles	**Time:** 1 hour
Time: 30 minutes	**Elevation change:** 400 feet
Elevation change: 125 feet	**Best lenses:** 28mm to 150mm

Directions: From Wellsboro, take US 6 west for 11.2 miles to Ansonia. Cross Marsh Creek and turn left onto Colton Road. Follow for 3.1 miles to a large parking area on the right. GPS coordinates: 41° 43.402′N, 77° 27.389′W

Y ou can expect Colton Point (Hike 50) to be crowded on summer weekends and especially so during peak autumn color. Because Barbour Rock
requires a walk of more than 100 yards, it will be almost empty, so I recommend this hike to avoid the crush of humanity.

Barbour Rock can be either a quick 1.1-mile loop or a longer 2.6-mile
loop, using the road as your return. Either is an enjoyable bit of hiking,
making for a great outing with kids. The Barbour Rock Loop Trail is shaped
like a tennis racket, with one short trail section leading to a loop around a
rocky knob.

Begin by crossing the road and walking down the gently rising blue-
blazed trail. At .23 mile, you come to a T intersection where the loop
begins. If you opt for the short 1.1-mile loop, your return will bring you in
from the right. Head straight and arrive at two fenced views of Barbour
Rock and a 100-foot-long series of ledges at .51 mile. The best view is at the
second south-facing fence. It's obvious that the short, wobbly wood fence
merely marks the view's location, so feel free to set up on the ledge
beyond. To complete the shorter loop, continue following the blue blazes,
rejoining the main trail at .72 mile. Turn left and arrive back at the parking
area at 1.1 miles.

For the longer 2.6-mile loop, from the second fenced Barbour Rock view
follow the orange-blazed West Rim Trail south. In 100 yards or so, you come
to a small stone platform sitting below the trail with a scruffy long-needle
pine near the head. The view, Vista 2, looks directly down into the gorge,
and I think this is better than the larger view area at Barbour Rock.

Continuing along the West Rim Trail, you'll find a footpath leading down
to a ledge at .6 mile. Although this ledge is accessible, I don't recommend

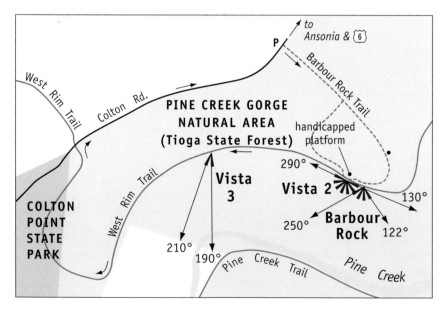

Barbour Rock. Heavy clouds and erratic fall color make for challenging shooting. In this case, I went with a longer lens to play with the curve of Pine Creek. *Canon EOS Rebel Xs, Tamron 28–200 at 150mm, Kodak E100VS, f/16 @ 1/2 sec.*

attempting it, as the loose clay slope is steep enough that any slip could prove disastrous, especially in damp conditions. Around .75 mile, the trail moves a dozen or so yards away from the rim and enters a small hemlock grove. Pine Creek's constant white-noise din is suddenly lost, and silence permeates the forest. The transition is so sudden that my wife and I walked back and forth several times to experience the effect, which is like a door closing. As we walked along on a subfreezing April morn, the drumming of downy woodpeckers echoed through the woods. When looking for food, they'll quietly pound into a tree, but when seeking mates in spring, males find hollow trees to drum on. Their persistent staccato beat is very loud, belying their tiny size.

After the quiet hemlock grove, a descending footpath is found at .8 mile on the left. This path provides a safe 10-foot descent to small pine-covered ledge at Vista 3. The pine cover makes a nice green foregound to contrast with fall color. In the distance is a classic view of overlapping ridges, with the sweeping curve of Pine Creek around Colton Point forming the middle ground.

The West Rim Trail continues close to the edge, and at 1.1 miles, hemlocks encroach on the left, clinging to unexposed ledges. At 1.22 miles, you come to a fire ring marking a campsite. There is no view here; rather, it's a delightfully quiet picnic spot. Farther along, the trail sweeps right away from the gorge at 1.5 miles. Here the trail is within sight and sound of Bear Run on the left all the way to the crossing of Colton Road at 2 miles. Turn right onto Colton Road, and return to your car at 2.6 miles.

Hike 52 Leonard Harrison State Park

Harrison Lookout

Type: cliff	**Field of view:** 210° to 360° at lower platform, 240° to 360° at upper platform
Rating: 5	**Relief:** 200 feet
GPS: 41° 41.704'N, 77° 27.342'W	**Elevation difference:** 707 feet
Faces: 285°	**Height:** 1,769 feet

Otter View

Type: ledge	**Field of view:** 180° to 240°
Rating: 5	**Relief:** 20 feet
GPS: 41° 41.502'N, 77° 27.371'W	**Elevation difference:** 499 feet
Faces: 210°	**Height:** 1,562 feet
Best times: any time	**Time:** 30 minutes
Difficulty: moderate; steep descent	**Elevation change:** 260 feet
Distance: Otter View, .6 mile	**Best lenses:** 20mm to 300mm

Directions: From Wellsboro, take PA 660 west for 11 miles to Leonard Harrison State Park. The route makes many turns and is well marked. GPS coordinates: 41° 41.800'N, 77° 27.283'W

Outdoor pioneer George Washington Sears wrote the first poems and verse describing Pine Creek Gorge under the pen name Nessmuk. Leonard Harrison State Park is perhaps the best known park in all the state. Summer visitation runs high, and the large parking area is packed during peak fall color weekends, which is why you want to get here on a weekday. The views are amazing.

Harrison Lookout is a series of view platforms connected by wide flights of stairs. The lowest platform provided views upstream and down, while the upper platform looks upstream. The stout high fence makes using a tripod difficult, so it's best to use the fence rail to support your camera.

During the summer, the best way to break up the monochromatic green gorge flanks is to shoot cloud shadows. This provides contrast to the scene, creating visual interest. Make sure you meter the sunlit ridges so the shadows go dark.

To get to Otter View, follow the Overlook Trail past the bathrooms, and bear right at .1 mile where the trail divides. You'll return on the left-hand section, which has a more reasonable ascent. The trail makes a steep descent, hanging near the cliff edge. At .3 mile, you come to a wooden view-

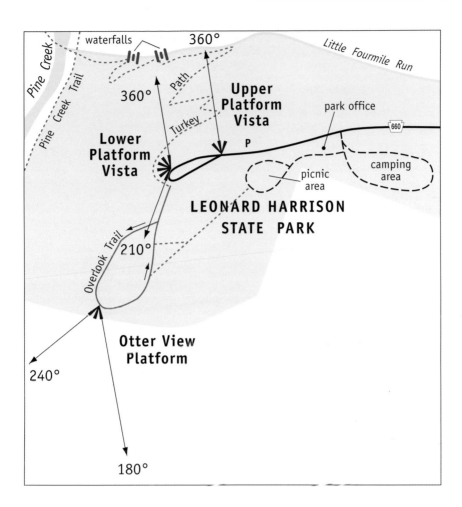

ing platform with an impressive exposure looking downstream. To return to your car, bear left away from the platform. The trail follows a broad drainage depression, and in spring you'll hear water tumbling over rocks. Although it's not the best bit of stream shooting around, when the water is flowing strong there are some nice macro compositions to be found.

Hike 53 | Band Rock, Tiadaghton State Forest

Type: cliff	**Height:** 1,743 feet
Rating: 4	**Best times:** late afternoon through sunset
GPS: 41° 31.254'N, 76° 56.751'W	**Difficulty:** easy
Faces: 270°	**Distance:** 1 mile
Field of view: 193° to 336°	**Time:** 30 minutes
Relief: 50 feet	**Elevation change:** 50 feet
Elevation difference: 885 feet	**Best lenses:** 17mm to 100mm

Directions: From the intersection of PA 14 and US 15 in Trout Run, take PA 14 east for 11.3 miles to the town of Ralston. Turn right onto Thompson Street, and in two blocks bear left to cross the railroad track. You are now on Rock Run Road and will cross Lycoming Creek on a new-looking concrete highway bridge. In .6 mile, bear left onto McIntyre Road, which starts out as good forest road but turns into a high-clearance drivable trail very quickly. Follow McIntyre Road for 3.9 miles to a parking area where the road is blocked by boulders. GPS coordinates: 41° 31.541'N, 76° 56.512'W

Band Rock. Notice how heavy cloud cover makes the image look flat and uninviting. Sometimes you have to take what you can get. *Canon EOS Rebel Xs, Tokina 20–35, 1-stop graduate, Kodak E100VS, f/27 @ 1/2 sec.*

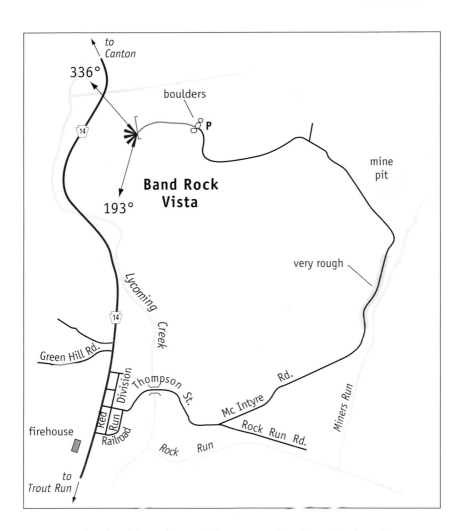

to
Canton

336°

boulders

P

14

mine
pit

Band Rock
Vista

193°

very rough

Lycoming Creek

14

Green Hill Rd.

Division

Thompson St.

Red Run

Railroad

Mc Intyre Rd.

Rock Run Rd.

Miners Run

firehouse

Rock Run

to
Trout Run

You used to be able to drive all the way to the viewpoint, but the amount of party mischief forced the Forest Service to block vehicle access. I guess the limit for hauling beer is half a mile. From the parking area, walk up the blocked woods road to the view, which is a 30-yard-wide cliff.

Looking down on the town of Ralston, you can easily see the narrow valley of Lycoming Creek, although you can't see the tributary creeks of Rock and Red Runs. New home construction in a looping meander in front of you replaced a charming farmette in 2005. My fear is that two large pasturelands on the far ridge will someday become vacation homes. Looking south beyond Ralston, you can follow Lycoming Creek's course by simply following the pattern overlapping ridge gaps.

Hike 54 Lambs Hill Picnic Area, Tioga State Forest

Type: ridge	**Elevation difference:** 904 feet
Rating: 5+	**Height:** 2,356 feet
GPS: 41° 41.408'N, 76° 51.987'W	**Best times:** sunrise through midmorning
Faces: 112°	**Trail:** none
Field of view: 65° to 158°	**Elevation change:** none
Relief: 5 feet	**Best lenses:** 50mm to 400mm

Directions: From the intersection of PA 414 and PA 14 in Canton, take PA 14 north for .5 mile and turn left on Upper Mountain Road. Follow for 4.5 miles, turning right onto Chapman/Lambs Road. In .3 mile, turn left into the Lambs Hill Picnic Area and park at the end of the road.

Located in an isolated eastern section of Tioga State Forest, Lambs Hill Picnic Area is the best eastern view in the region, and the never-ending valley view is must-shoot dawn location. Hills dotting the valley make for

Farm Ponds. A long lens means everything when you want to reach into a scene and shoot patterns. *Canon EOS Digital Rebel, Tamron 200–400, polarizer, ISO100 setting, f/16 @ .6 sec.*

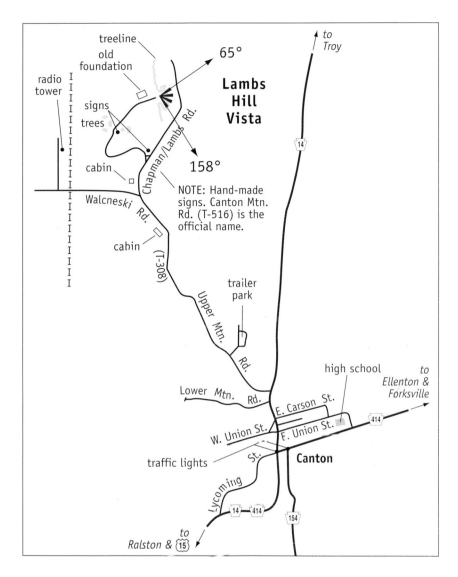

radio
tower

treeline

old
foundation

signs

trees

cabin

Walcneski Rd.

cabin

Chapman/Lambs Rd.

(T-308)

65°

**Lambs
Hill
Vista**

158°

NOTE: Hand-made
signs. Canton Mtn.
Rd. (T-516) is the
official name.

to
Troy

14

Upper Mtn. Rd.

trailer
park

Lower Mtn. Rd.

high school

to
Ellenton &
Forksville

E. Carson St.

414

W. Union St.

E. Union St.

traffic lights

St.

Canton

Lycoming

14　414

154

to
Ralston & 15

incredible graphic forms, and farm ponds add little patches of fog on chilly
mornings. The best way to shoot here is to park your vehicle near the
brushy edge of the view cutout and climb on the roof. This gives you up to
another 10 feet of relief, eliminating all foreground issues.

Being so isolated, this location makes for a good party spot, as evidenced
by all the broken glass. Don't be surprised if you wake some hungover ille-
gal campers on weekend summer mornings.

Hike 55 Sharp Top, Tiadaghton State Forest

Type: ridge	**Elevation difference:** 800 feet
Rating: 5	**Height:** 2,000 feet
GPS: 41° 28.300'N, 76° 50.883'W	**Best times:** sunrise through midmorning, late afternoon through sunset
Faces: 160°	**Trail:** none
Field of view: 90° to 240°	**Elevation change:** none
Relief: 10 feet	**Best lenses:** 35mm to 150mm

Directions: From the intersection of PA 14 and US 15 in Trout Run, take PA 14 east for 8.6 miles, and turn right on Pleasant Stream Road at the village of Marsh Hill. Follow for 10.1 miles, entering state forest lands. Make a hard right onto Hillsgrove Road, which climbs quickly, and make the first right onto John Merrell Road, which has trees and brush very close to or overhanging the road. After 2.8 miles, turn left at a T intersection to continue on John Merrell, which dead-ends at the view in .1 mile.

This dead-end forest has a gloriously wide view of a hilly valley cradled by Burnett Ridge (which you're on) and Cove Mountain 4.6 miles away. With such a wide view, there's no reason not to linger here through every kind of light, from full moon illumination to midday. Two valleys split Cove Mountain. The one to your left contains the village of Proctor, and the one on the right is a dividing drainage holding Bar Bottom Hollow, near the village of Wallis Run. Between these two, almost unnoticeable as a simple ridge gap, is the hidden valley of PA 87 and the Loyalsock Creek north of Smiths Knob. The only things restricting your compositions are two white houses sitting close in at 196° and 183°, almost hidden by a large tree. Just be aware of them and keep them out of the frame. Other than that, the sky is truly the limit here.

One pleasant summer evening when I came to shoot moonrise, I had a chance to observe bat feeding behaviors. After the sky had darkened to the point where I couldn't shoot anymore, I saw several bats and numerous insects silhouetted against the sky. I became fascinated by how nimble bats are. As an insect hovered into view, a bat would wheel around to pick it out of the sky. I could see how the bats pulled their wings in to form an umbrella and scoop the insects out of the air with great ease. I must have spent an hour just watching them, until I could no longer see them against the sky. When I turned on my headlamp, bugs began to gather in the beam, and as expected, a bat zipped in just inches from my face. It was very cool to see one snatch a large moth with its mouth only inches from my face.

What, No Tea? For all its beauty, Sharp Top is a challenging location. With fog filling the valley, I decided to put my wife in the picture, her red coat standing out against the green foliage. Even in August, it can get chilly in the mountains. *Canon EOS Digital Rebel, Tokina 20–35, polarizer, ISO100 setting, f/16 @ 2 sec.*

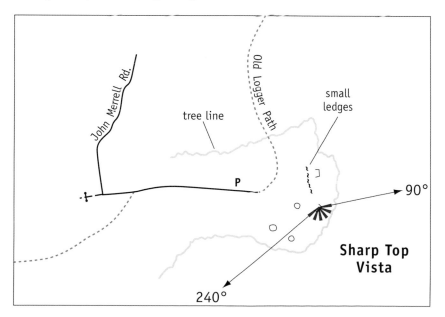

Hike 56 Old Loggers Path, Sullivan Mountain, Tiadaghton State Forest

Vista 1

Type: ledge	Field of view: 235° to 269°
Rating: 4+	Relief: 20 feet
GPS: 41° 32.250'N, 76° 53.085'W	Elevation difference: 617 feet
Faces: 265°	Height: 1,874 feet

Vista 2

Type: ledge	Field of view: 265° to 352°
Rating: 4	Relief: 30 feet
GPS: 41° 30.638'N, 76° 54.299'W	Elevation difference: 988 feet
Faces: 310°	Height: 1,987 feet

Vista 3

Type: ledge	Field of view: 118° to 195°
Rating: 4	Relief: 30 feet
GPS: 41° 30.423'N, 76° 54.121'W	Elevation difference: 1,005 feet
Faces: 155°	Height: 2,134 feet

Vista 4

Type: ledge	Field of view: 52° to 132°
Rating: 3	Relief: 20 feet
GPS: 41° 30.505'N, 77° 53.935'W	Elevation difference: 974 feet
Faces: 90°	Height: 2,103 feet
Best times: any time is good, but early morning is best	Time: 3 hours, 30 minutes
Difficulty: moderate	Elevation change: 750 feet
Distance: 7.9 miles	Best lenses: 50mm to 200mm

Directions: From Forksville at the intersection of PA 154 and PA 87, take PA 154 west for 10 miles through Estella and Lincoln Falls to the village of Shunk. In Shunk, where PA 154 turns right, proceed straight on SR 4002 toward Tomkins Corner and Ellenton for 3.7 miles. In the village of Ellenton, at a Y intersection, bear left onto the gravel Ellenton/Pleasant Stream Road (SR 1013). Proceed 1.1 miles and bear right at the next Y onto Ellenton Ridge/Yellow Dog Road. Drive 3.2 miles to where Ellenton Ridge Road makes a right at a gated road (your hiking return route), becoming Yellow Dog Road. Continue downhill for .6 mile to where the Old Loggers Path crosses the road. Park in a large wide spot on the right. GPS coordinates: 41° 31.874'N, 76° 52.368'W

If you have kids that are old enough to tolerate up to four hours in the woods, then bring them along, because this is a great family hike with pleasant trails, nice views, and delightful bogs to explore. The Old Loggers Path (OLP) is a 27-mile loop trail. This hike uses about 4 miles of it plus a couple of old woods roads to form a figure-eight loop hike. If you're coming for afternoon shooting, follow the route as described. If it's dawn or morning light, then park .6 mile up the road, where Ellenton Ridge/Yellow Dog Road turned right at the gated road, and run the route backward.

From the parking area, cross the road to follow the orange-blazed OLP north. Using an old rail grade, the OLP holds a level line while Yellow Dog Road falls away. At .55 mile, cross a pipeline cut where you can hear water coming from the confluence of Hawk and Rock Runs. The OLP sweeps left at .8 mile along Sullivan Mountain's flank. Just after, you come to a blue-blazed side trail for the first vista at .9 mile. Arrows and signs direct you downslope a dozen yards to a wonderful view of Rock Run valley.

If you look along the valley's axis from the south side, Rock Run's glen appears as a winding depression. Directly ahead is a shadow line, like a fabric crease, indicating Hounds Run, which has a fine waterfall. From the upper set of rocks, work down through the scrubby black birch to a series of boulders ending at a large drop. From here most of the foreground issues are eliminated.

Return to the OLP and turn right, following the wide, level grade. At 1.9 miles, turn left up another road, thus avoiding a steep drop into Doe Run. Paralleling the run for 50 yards, cross a small tributary at a campsite on the left. At 2 miles, turn right to cross Doe Run. From here the OLP parallels Doe Run again, passing another campsite directly across from the last one before swinging left away from the run at 2.08 miles. This entire sequence of turns is well marked with double blazes and arrows.

On the old rail grade once again, you'll find that the cinders underfoot make surprisingly warm hiking for the next several hundred yards. Bear left uphill off the rail grade at 2.9 miles, passing through a series of car-size conglomerate blocks called Big Rocks. Now paralleling Buck Run, you'll pop out onto a meadow road at a T intersection at 3.5 miles. This is the Stoney Trail/Ellenton Grade. To the left is your return to Ellenton Ridge Road, and to the right the OLP continues. Turn right, crossing the rocky head of Buck Run in a few yards. You'll come to the yellow-gated Crandall Town Road Trail on the left at 3.65 miles. This will be part of your return route. (For sunrise at Vistas 3 and 4, turn left here when coming in along the Stoney/Ellenton Grade Trails.)

Shortly after passing the Crandall Town Trail at 3.8 miles, you pass a large boulder on the left and some double blazes announcing that the OLP turns left off the road grade. Climbing easily at first, then steeply, the OLP follows part of a rock slide before bearing right at 3.88 miles into a mountain laurel grove. Pass by a narrow view at 4 miles, proceeding to a series of larger ledges at 4.1 miles, which is Vista 2.

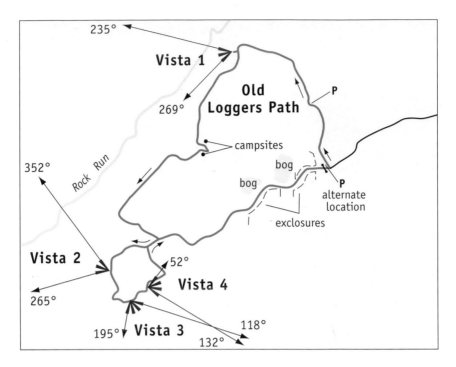

There are two sets of ledges here, one a true ledge and the other a yet-to-be-cleaved block of conglomerate. Both perches are excellent with wide fields of view, but the second ledge has a better west exposure. Sunsets between May and August will be in frame from both spots. You can make out the Hounds Run drainage ahead of you, and Miners Run is on the left almost out of view. Black birch saplings linger close from both views, so take the time to carefully check the bottom of your frame for "sneakers."

Climbing away from the view, you pass through a large fernery. You may not have noticed, but the OLP has been making a long, meandering left around Sullivan Mountain's nose, arriving at the third vista at 4.6 miles. This one is made up of two high ledges looking southeast over Pleasant Stream Valley, facing Potash Mountain. Although the ledges provide a lot of relief, a .2-mile-wide plateau separates the view from the steep-sided valley, giving this location a more bucolic look. The lefthand ledge is better than the right, because it looks into Sixth Bottom Hollow.

After you leave this vista, a short section of spongy moss covers the OLP, giving your tired feet a short break. At 4.84 miles, you come to an L-shaped orange arrow painted on a rock where the OLP makes a hard left. Bushwhack straight ahead for a couple yards to a large boulder promontory marking the fourth and final vista. Facing more easterly than the last view, this vista looks farther up Pleasant Stream, with Sixth Bottom Hollow and Long Run dividing the otherwise flat forest terrain into three humps. This location is the best sunrise spot.

Twilight. The setting sun creates deep shadows along one side of a valley that won't render on camera. The solution is easy—just wait for the sun to go down. *Canon EOS Digital Rebel, Tamron 28–200, polarizer, 2-stop graduate, 10CC magenta, ISO100 setting, f/8 @ .5 sec.*

Return to the L-shaped arrow and turn right (north). Shortly after, make a steep but short descent, arriving at a campsite and a large hemlock with orange arrows at 5.1 miles. The Crandall Town Road Trail and the OLP join here. As you face the fire ring, the Crandall Town Road Trail enters from the far right and leaves to your left. The OLP exits the campsite on another road, also to your right. Turn left onto the Crandall Town Road Trail, which is wide but somewhat overgrown with ferns. After a long loop around Sullivan

Mountain's nose, it's surprising to find that it's just a quarter mile back to the yellow gate on the Ellenton Grade, at 5.36 miles. Turn right, arriving back at the head of Buck Run at 5.44 miles. Here the OLP turns left but you go straight, following the woods road.

Climbing slightly, the wide road is damp in places, and the surrounding forest alternates between pine and hardwood. At 6 miles, you'll note that the forest floor changes texture as more upland bogs become noticeable. Cross the pipeline again at 6.37 mile, at the beginning of the deer exclosure on the right. When the exclosure becomes hidden by pines, look for a large meadow on the left. Should the vista conditions be less than ideal, work the meadow until you run out of film or memory space. With lots of large standing snags, this upland meadow is a haven for birds and mammals. I explored several drainage channels that were filled with cold, clean water even during August's heat. A couple deep pools I found had turtles and frogs sunning themselves. It's hard to explain how nice this location is; it's simply fantastic. Another meadow is on the right, marked by an old wooden sign announcing the Long Run Trail. Where this trail goes is not clear.

Another exclosure appears on the left near 7 miles. At 7.24 miles, you come to the yellow gate at the Ellenton Ridge/Yellow Dog Road turn you passed on the drive in. Turn left, heading down the gravel Yellow Dog Road, alternating from left to right so that you keep to the outside of any turns. At 7.67 miles, the OLP joins the road from the right, and at 7.9 miles, you arrive back at your car.

Hike 57 Allegheny Ridge, Loyalsock Trail, Wyoming State Forest

Type: ledge	**Height:** 1,883 feet
Rating: 5 when cut back, 2 when not	**Best times:** early morning through evening
GPS: 41° 20.460′N, 76° 51.771′W	**Difficulty:** difficult
Faces: 188°	**Distance:** 3.7 miles
Field of view: 160° to 210°	**Time:** 2 hours
Relief: 20 feet	**Elevation change:** 1,120 feet
Elevation difference: 1,110 feet	**Best lenses:** 50mm to 175mm

Directions: From the intersection of PA 154 and PA 87 in Forksville, take PA 87 south for 14.3 miles and turn left on Little Bear Road. Proceed .9 mile and park on the right in a wide spot adjacent to the forest district maintenance shed access bridge. GPS coordinates: 41° 21.379′N, 76° 51.515′W

This hike takes you to one of the few mountain views from the massive scarp of the Allegheny Front. Extending in a broad arc from Wyoming County to Somerset County, the Allegheny Front marks the point where the terrain begins to slope in the general direction of Lakes Erie and Ontario. This massive feature is the remains of a mountain outwash plain laid down during all four of Pennsylvania's mountain-building phases, the last of which was the Alleghenian Orogeny, ending 220 million years ago.

Because of heavy undergrowth within a steep boulder fall or defile, this hike takes some effort to navigate during the first half mile. Although challenging, this difficulty is what gives this hike its charm, so to speak. You really have to want to get to this view.

Begin by crossing the bridge into the district maintenance area and bear left between the two sheds, following the yellow-and-red-blazed Loyalsock Trail (LT). You are now on the combined LT and Peter's Path. The LT climbs along a rocky woods road, crossing a small stream in .17 mile, after which it departs the road and becomes a footpath. Here you pass through a heavily overgrown section of about 100 yards.

As you enter a small valley, take a moment to survey the terrain. There are a large number of blowdowns, and the lack of mature tree cover has allowed the understory to run rampant. This section is frustrating to navigate, as blazes are few and the footpath not entirely clear, but thankfully it doesn't last long. Afterward, however, is a wide draw filled with boulders

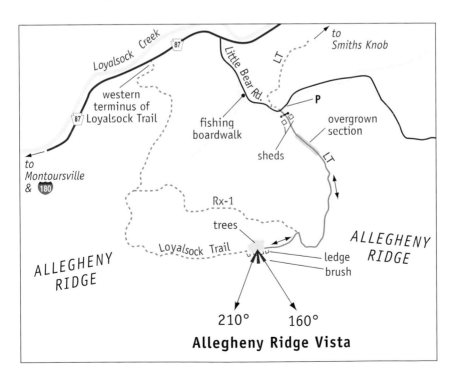

Allegheny Ridge Vista

Dodging Raindrops. Hand-holding a camera over your head is always an option when you need elevation to eliminate foreground problems. *Canon EOS Digital Rebel, Tokina 20–35, polarizer, ISO200 setting, f/8 @ $^1/_{60}$ sec.*

and stinging nettles galore. This is the section I call "charming." There are times when a challenging trail section is a royal pain, yet somehow this was actually fun. It was hot, humid, and generally miserable when I did this climb, yet I had a keen sense of satisfaction when I got through it. What's interesting is what you see when you stop to look around. The valley walls have slid into the valley bowl. If you look carefully at the extent of the slide area, you simply have to be in awe of the power required to move this amount of rock. Considering the adjacent tree growth, I'd estimate the slide is around fifty years old.

After you've wrestled through rocks, boulders, and nettles, the LT jogs right out of the drainage you've been following at .5 mile near a massive hemlock. The rocks aren't gone; they're just less numerous now. As you pass by LT mile marker 4, the trail's pitch slackens. Turn right onto a woods road at a T intersection at 1.3 miles. Ample blazes mark the turn, and a multiuse trail joins from the left where the LT is marked with a Horses Not Permitted sign. Shortly after, the LT bears right to head uphill, marked by several directional signs. After a brief climb, you come to a T intersection with a red-X connector trail at 1.5 miles. The red-X trail follows the woods road, rejoining the LT in 1.35 miles. Turn left to stay with the LT, climbing steadily again. The LT soon tops out on the crest of Allegheny Ridge, then turns right to follow the scarp, which is never farther than several dozen yards to the left.

You arrive at a short side trail to the view at 1.85 miles. The view area is rather tight, and the best position is from higher up. Bald Eagle Mountain is the large ridge in the distance, sitting 8.6 miles away. It marks the northern-most fold of the Ridge and Valley Province and the limit of view. The best way to shoot this location is by holding your camera overhead, thus gaining height above the foreground scrub. When cut back, this view is incredible, but when it's not, it's so-so at best. Regardless, it's worth the effort to get to so you can make your own judgment.

You can create a loop hike by continuing along the LT to where it con-nects with the red-X trail at 3.75 miles; then turn right onto that trail, rejoin-ing the LT at 5.1 miles. I recommend instead reversing your route, arriving back at your car at 3.7 miles.

Hike 58 Rider Park, Lycoming County

Vista 1

Type: ridge	**Field of view:** 50° to 90°
Rating: 3–4	**Relief:** 5 feet
GPS: 41° 20.465'N, 76° 55.651'W	**Elevation difference:** 844 feet
Faces: 70°	**Height:** 1,499 feet

Vista 2

Type: ridge	**Field of view:** 158° to 243°
Rating: 4	**Relief:** 20 feet
GPS: 41° 20.467'N, 76° 56.017'W	**Elevation difference:** 777 feet
Faces: 200°	**Height:** 1,503 feet
Best times: early morning through evening	**Time:** 1 hour
Difficulty: easy	**Elevation change:** 346 feet
Distance: 2.1 miles	**Best lenses:** 35mm to 200mm

Directions: From the PA 87/US 220/I-180 interchange at Montoursville, take PA 87 north for 4.4 miles, and turn left onto PA 973 west. Follow for 1.9 miles to the village of Warrensville, and turn right onto Pleasant Valley Road (SR 2022). In just under .9 mile, turn right on Caleb Road; the sign may be hidden by a tree. Follow the paved then gravel road for 1.6 miles to a large dead-end parking area. GPS coordinates: 41° 20.831'N, 76° 56.205'W

This quick woods road trail takes you to the best view from the massive scarp of the Allegheny Front. From the parking area, walk away from the sign kiosk and around the yellow gate to follow the yellow-blazed Katy Jane Trail. This wide trail uses an old woods road to climb out of a hanging valley. Near .16 mile, another woods road exits right, but stick with the yellow blazes and continue ahead. After a steady climb, you'll arrive at the first vista, a pretty good view of the Loyalsock Valley on the left at .7 mile. Even though it is slowly overgrowing, this is the best view of the Loyalsock where it turns to exit the Allegheny Plateau for the Ridge and Valley Province. In the middle distance is a large and prominent hump, which is Smith's Knob.

The Katy Jane Trail bears right to follow the ridge front. To the left are several ledges that jut out into the tree cover below. These rocks mark the southernmost edge of the Allegheny Front, which is the exposed face of the plateau. The level trail makes one hard left near the second vista, which you

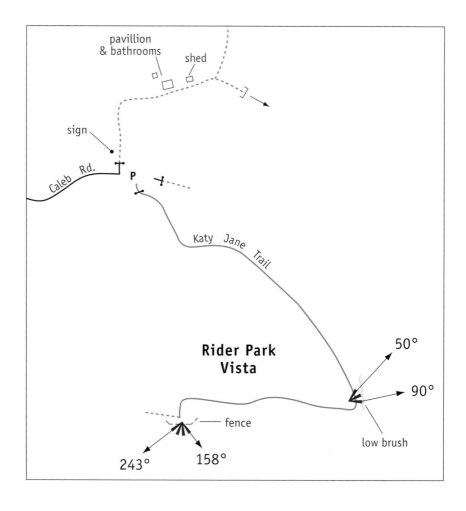

Encroachment. Looking left over the large humps that hide Loyalsock Creek, you can see development creeping in on the right. *Canon EOS Digital Rebel, Tokina 20–35, polarizer, 1-stop graduate, ISO200 setting, f/8 @ $^1/_{50}$ sec.*

reach at 1.05 miles. This fenced exposure is the best view along the entire front, which runs from Somerset County all the way to Wilkes-Barre.

As with most views like it, where you set up will determine the field of view. Standing on the right provides a splendid view of several large hills south of Loyalsockville, which hide Montoursville and I-180. Standing on the left, you look off toward Williamsport, which is also hidden by large hills. Enjoy this southwest view while it lasts. Many houses are being built in the valley below, which I find unfortunate. The large ridge looming 9 miles to the south is Bald Eagle Mountain, which is the northernmost ridge of the Ridge and Valley Province. A gap in the ridge is where US 15 cuts through a large, open fold near the ridge's eastern terminus.

Hike 59 Upper and Lower Alpine Views, Loyalsock Trail, Wyoming State Forest

Upper Alpine

Type: ridge	Field of view: visto
Rating: 2	Relief: 10 feet
GPS: 41° 27.619'N, 76° 37.982'W	Elevation difference: 853 feet
Faces: 280°	Height: 1,758 feet

Lower Alpine

Type: cliff	Field of view: 198° to 338°
Rating: 5	Relief: 200 feet
GPS: 41° 27.732'N, 76° 38.207'W	Elevation difference: 557 feet
Faces: 285°	Height: 1,462 feet
Best times: late afternoon through sunset	Time: 1 hour
Difficulty: moderate; steep climb on the return	Elevation change: 380 feet
Distance: 2 miles	Best lenses: 17mm to 125mm

Directions: From the Worlds End State Park Visitor Center, turn left onto PA 154 East and proceed .4 mile to a Y intersection with Double Run Road (SR 3009). Bear right up the steep hill, and follow Double Run Road south for 2.1 miles to the second intersection of Coal Mine Road. Turn right onto Coal Mine Road, and proceed 2 miles to a large parking area on the left near where the Loyalsock Trail crosses the road. GPS coordinates: 41° 27.399'N, 76° 37.753'W

From the parking area, walk along Coal Mine Road a short distance to where the red-and-yellow-blazed Loyalsock Trail (LT) crosses. Turn left into a small hemlock grove, following the LT along the gorge's rim. At .32 mile, you come to a grassy meadow and Upper Alpine View. (There's a blue-and-yellow sign nailed to a tree.) Looking out upon the Loyalsock Valley between Forksville and Hillsgrove, you can make out a couple of farms, although black birches now crowd the view.

Shortly after, the LT makes a steep descent as it loops left. When it bottoms out, it runs parallel to the section 260 feet above. Now at .9 mile, the LT turns right toward daylight and begins to run close to a series of ledges. At .98 mile, an opening near what looks like a small ledge appears. Bypass this small false view, and look for a long fissure perhaps 80 yards long separating an exposed ledge from the wider plateau. This announces the large opening of Lower Alpine View, which is at 1 mile.

With nearly 200 feet of relief, this cliff is one of the best vantage points in Sullivan County. The Loyalsock Valley is rather wide here, and a small home close in can be cropped from view to create an organic image. What I love

Lower Alpine View. Glowing leaves anchor the foreground and help offset the large expanse of dark foliage filling the valley. *Tachihara 4x5 field camera, 150mm Schneider Symmar f/5.6, polarizer, 2-stop graduate, 81A warming filter, 6x7 roll film back, Kodak E100VS, f/32 @ 1 sec.*

about this spot is watching cloud shadows dappling the valley with interesting shapes.

Complete your hike by reversing your route. Keep in mind that the steep climb out will take almost two-thirds of your hiking time.

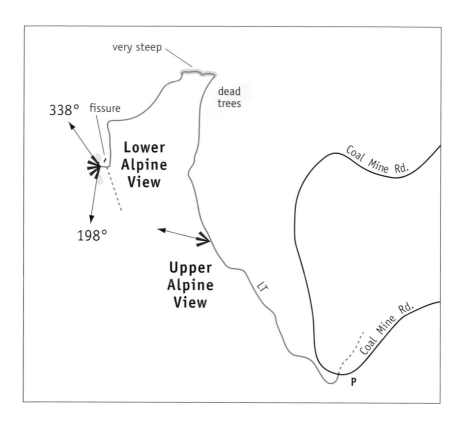

Hike 60 Kettle Creek Gorge, Loyalsock Trail, Wyoming State Forest

Type: cliff	**Height:** 1,499 feet
Rating: 4	**Best times:** afternoon through sunset
GPS: 41° 24.523'N, 76° 40.279'W	**Difficulty:** moderate; one steep climb and descent
Faces: 278°	**Distance:** 5.2 miles
Field of view: 265° to 300°	**Time:** 2 hours
Relief: 40 feet	**Elevation change:** 1,170 feet
Elevation difference: 418 feet	**Best lenses:** 17mm to 100mm

Directions: From the intersection of PA 87 and PA 154 in Forksville, take PA 87 south for 9.8 miles and turn left onto Ogdonia Road. You may see a sign for Camp Lycogis on the right. Follow Ogdonia Road for 3 miles to a Y intersection with Brunnerdale Road. Bear left onto Brunnerdale and continue .3 mile, parking in a large area on the left adjacent to a big culvert. GPS coordinates: 41° 23.118'N, 76° 40.141'W

One of the challenges in creating this guide was fighting the clock. Sunrise and sunset wait for nobody, and the pressure to cover as much ground as possible is enormous when your subject is the entire state. With my week's task list complete, this ended up being the only hike planned for the day. Without any constraints, I was able to enjoy a quiet afternoon wandering around chasing bird sounds, examining snakes, and lying down eye-to-eye with a tolerant turtle that didn't seem to mind me trying to commune with it. In short, this was a really fun trail.

Begin by locating the red-and-yellow-blazed Loyalsock Trail (LT) adjacent to the culvert, and follow Ogdonia Creek downstream, keeping the creek on your left. Passing through whispering pines and across comfortable loamy soil, the LT gradually moves away from Ogdonia Creek and at .4 mile turns right, heading uphill on an old woods road, then switches back left at .53 mile. For a time the LT is level before turning right at .7 mile to climb again. Another left onto a woods road occurs at .83 mile, then a jog right at .9 mile. You arrive at a sign for Angel Falls at 1.1 miles. If you have time, visit Angel Falls on the return trip, which will add .1 mile to your total hike and includes a difficult descent.

Deep Valley. By stepping back from the view, you can use trees to create a frame for the scene. *Canon EOS Digital Rebel, Tokina 20–35, polarizer, 1-stop graduate, ISO100 setting, f/8 @ ¹/20 sec.*

The forest has changed somewhat in the 400-foot climb to this point. In the valley below, the rich soil supports larger trees of both soft- and hardwood species. As you climbed, rock ledges were close to the surface, and the soil was much drier and lacked nutrients. Even though the trees here and

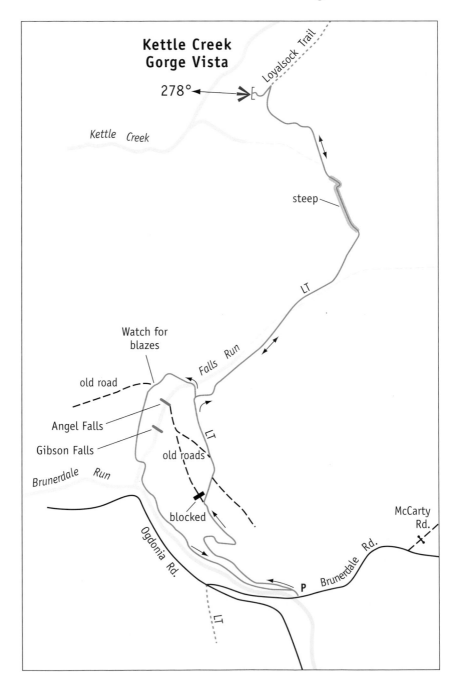

below are the same age, the specimens at this elevation are smaller, and the forest is less dense.

Another short climb follows, after which you turn left to cross Falls Run at 1.5 miles. As the LT leaves Falls Run behind you, climb yet again; then make a sharp left at LT mile marker 24, which is at 1.84 miles. Soon you arrive at the high point for the hike, now 1.94 miles from your car and 660 feet higher. From here it's 510 feet downhill to the view. A long, steep, meandering descent follows, with some sections of loose rock that can send you sprawling, should you move too quickly. The LT finally levels out at 2.5 miles. Ahead is a large blue sign indicating the blue-blazed view trail to the left. It's only a short walk of 50 yards through open woods. Some blazes are hard to locate, so just head toward daylight above a large stone slab.

Kettle Creek Vista faces almost due west and allows for shooting at any time of day. Late-afternoon shadows mask the north ridge, requiring careful exposure, so it's best to get here while sunlight still fills the gorge. The only true sunset shot is during the few days near the equinoxes when the sun sets along 280°, the autumnal being the best. In summer, sunsets will be far to the right, plunging the north ridge in shadow an hour before.

As I approached the view, a crow bolted from a nearby tree and flew over the precipice. It in turn scared up a red-tailed hawk sitting on the cliff. The hawk circled for a time, screaming its distinct high-pitched *screeeee* before moving on. Next a hummingbird hovered near my face, apparently admiring my bright yellow shirt, then zipped away to sit in a nearby tree. After a few moments, it came back to confirm that I wasn't a flower and zipped off again into the open air. As I grabbed my camera out of the pack, a small snake slithered quickly over my boots, moved away, and coiled up at the base of a tree, where it warily watched me. I decided it didn't want me to lie down and commune with it the way I had with the turtle in Falls Run. These simple joys are why you must throw on some boots and get into the woods.

To return to your car, reverse your route to the sign for Angel Falls, now at 4.1 miles. For a straight shot back to your car, continue along the LT, returning to your car at 5.2 miles. If you'd like to visit the falls, turn right to descend on the prominently blue-blazed trail, arriving at the falls head .3 mile after the turn (now 4.4 miles total). I find that returning to the LT is just one climb too many, so I recommend heading downhill from the falls head, keeping well away from the steep ledges flanking Falls Run. Pick your way down the difficult steep slope to where it bottoms out and turn left, heading for the creek. Another falls, called Gibson, sits below Angel Falls near the hill's base. Cross the creek at a convenient point, and with it now on the right, follow the run all the way to Ogdonia Creek, arriving at 4.65 miles. Turn left, keeping Ogdonia Creek on your right, and follow it to the culvert next to the parking area. You'll pick up the LT in the last 50 yards, arriving back at your car at 5.3 miles.

Hike 61 High Knob Overlook, Wyoming State Forest

Type: ridge	**Elevation difference:** 1,006 feet
Rating: 5	**Height:** 1,978 feet
GPS: 41° 26.687'N, 76° 40.749'W	**Best times:** late afternoon through sunset
Faces: 250°	**Trail:** none
Field of view: 180° to 320°	**Elevation change:** none
Relief: 5 feet	**Best lenses:** 28mm to 400mm

Directions: From Worlds End State Park at PA 154 and Double Run Road (SR 3009), head south on Double Run Road for 2.8 miles to High Knob Road, where a large sign marking the vista is on the right. Turn right onto the paved High Knob. After 2.3 miles, when the unpaved Dry Run Road comes in from the left, bear right, staying on the paved High Knob Road. Follow it for 2.5 miles to the vista, which is a loop road.

You can just park the car and shoot sunset here—it's that easy. High Knob is a very popular sunset location, but the lot is large and the view area wide, so there should be no problem finding a nice spot. Even though the vista looks right into Hillsgrove, you can't see the village, PA 87, or the Loyalsock Creek, which makes this a perfect location. Visible as a large, round knob directly ahead at 1.4 miles is Round Knob, which sits above Hillsgrove. A wide bowl beyond it is a dry drainage flanked by Gooseberry Hill. A large gap on the left is where the Loyalsock Creek loops through the ridge toward the village of Barbours. These hills are spectacular in fall color.

To avoid crowds, try shooting full moonset during sunrise. Also, if you follow the loop road past the parking area for about .4 mile, you'll come to a

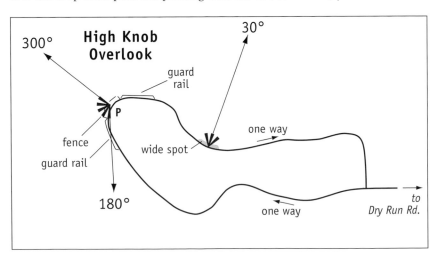

wide alley through the trees on the left. This vista, which faces 30°, looks down onto a bridge over the Loyalsock Creek north of Hillsgrove. It's only a long-lens shot, but it's worth a few moments to check it out.

Hike 62 Canyon Vista, Wyoming State Forest

Type: ridge	**Elevation difference**: 650 feet
Rating: 4	**Height**: 1,772 feet
GPS: 41° 27.757'N, 76° 34.469'W	**Best times**: midmorning through sunset
Faces: 330°	**Trail**: none
Field of view: left side, 270° to 30°; right side, 300° to 50°	**Elevation change**: 30 feet
Relief: 5 feet	**Best lenses**: 35mm to 200mm

Directions: From Worlds End State Park at PA 154 and Double Run Road (SR 3009), take PA 154 east .6 mile toward the campground area. There are two rights off of PA 154. Take the first, Mineral Spring Road, which has a sign for Canyon Vista. If you miss it, turn around at the second, which is the campground entrance. Follow Mineral Spring for 1.4 miles to where Cold Run Road joins at a shallow angle from the left. Make a hard left onto Cold Run and follow for .8 mile to the parking area and the view. GPS coordinates: 41° 27.757'N, 76° 34.469'W

Although pictures from Canyon Vista have graced countless magazine covers, wall calendars, and perhaps every *Endless Mountains* travel guide ever published, Canyon Vista is a tight place to work. The view is grand, but a fence and mature hemlock trees lining the view make finding the perfect setup a challenge. From the base of the stairs, look for a wide gap between two large trees a little to the right. This position works best when the weeds in front of the fence are well trimmed, and it's the best place to shoot into Loyalsock Canyon near the swimming area.

Thunderstorm Approaching. In the dull haze of August heat, it can be hard to shoot sunset. Here a brewing thunderstorm put a hint of color into the sky. *Canon EOS Digital Rebel, Tokina 20–35, polarizer, 2-stop graduate, ISO100 setting, f/8 @ .3 sec.*

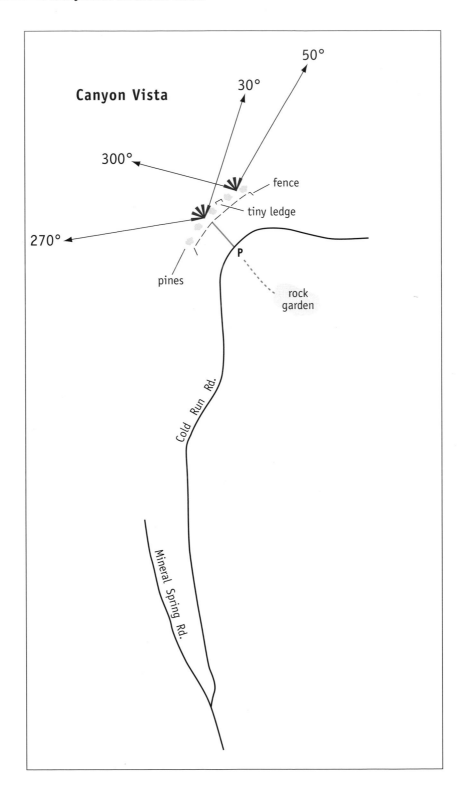

Canyon Vista

50°

30°

300°

fence

tiny ledge

270°

pines

P

rock
garden

Cold Run Rd.

Mineral Spring Rd.

In view below is the intersection of Dry Run and PA 154, and the double yellow line and stop sign are clearly visible in the viewfinder. Take great care to keep them out of the frame. A normal to slight telephoto eliminates that problem and helps avoid overhanging hemlock branches. Another consideration when shooting around midday is a white building sitting above and beyond the third ridge from you. Carefully examine your viewfinder to make sure this potential highlight won't ruin the final image.

The next large tree gap to the right is another good spot with a more northerly view. I like Canyon Vista for sunset or when light fog or mist fills the canyon, as either conceals foreground problems and adds a nice texture to an otherwise confining viewpoint.

Hike 63 **Table Rock, Appalachian Trail**

Type: ledge	**Height:** 1,330 feet
Rating: 3	**Best times:** sunrise through midmorning, late afternoon
GPS: 40° 25.296'N, 76° 53.684'W	**Difficulty:** easy; woods road and few rocks
Faces: 157°	**Distance:** 4 miles
Field of view: 104° to 210°	**Time:** 2 hours
Relief: 50 feet	**Elevation change:** 160 feet
Elevation difference: 933 feet	**Best lenses:** 20mm to 300mm

Directions: From the I-81/US 322 interchange on the north side of Harrisburg, take US 322/22 west toward Dauphin. In 5 miles, exit onto PA 225 north (Dauphin and Halafax). Shortly after you exit, PA 225 makes a left; follow the signs. In less than 2 miles, when PA 325 enters from the right, continue on PA 225. As PA 225 begins to climb Peters Mountain, you'll need to slow down near the ridge crest. The Appalachian Trail (AT) crosses the highway on a footbridge high above the road. As soon as this bridge is in sight, look for a small, steep gravel lane on the right. Turn right and follow the short lane to a large gravel parking area. If you miss the turn, don't try to turn around in a cottage driveway just beyond the AT footbridge. A U-turn here is blind and an invitation to disaster with southbound traffic. Instead, continue down the mountain for 1.5 miles, and make a U-turn at the first road you see on the left, T 547. GPS coordinates: 40° 24.706'N, 76° 55.796'W

A name like Table Rock makes you expect a massive level slab of stone. Large yes, level no. Table Rock is a substantial piece of conglomerate measuring 20 by 35 feet, with the long axis pitched down so that the slab sits nearly vertical. Photographically speaking, the view is OK. It is best suited for fall, as the middle ground is dominated by the flank of Third Mountain, sitting just 1.5 miles across the narrow valley of Clark's Creek.

Barn in Fog. In summer, the sun rises along the valley axis, sending shafts of light deep into the valley. Ground fog rising around this barn glows, creating magical pictures. The high ISO setting makes grainy images, which works well in this instance. *Canon EOS Digital Rebel, Tamron 200–400, polarizer, ISO800 setting, f/16 @ ¹/100 sec.*

From the parking area, look for the white-blazed Appalachian Trail exiting the corner opposite the footbridge. There are three large, uneven steps dropping from the parking lot to the trail. From this point to the view, the trail is fairly straight and rises and falls repeatedly in 20- or 30-foot humps. The first 100-yard stretch is rather close to the mountain's edge. At around .4 mile, a woods road joins from the left. This is the same road that exited from the back of the parking area and is the access road to an antenna array that the Appalachian Trail just looped around. You'll be on this road until you cross a power line at .6 mile. When you get to the power-line cut, you may want to drop your gear and climb through the boulders to the ridgetop to get a sense of what Table Rock will look like.

At .75 mile, the trail reaches a relative low point, and from here to the view it's an undulating series of short climbs. Table Rock comes into view at 2 miles. Turn right onto a short blue-blazed trail and you'll reach Table Rock in about 50 feet. As you gaze out on the view, a couple things will jump out

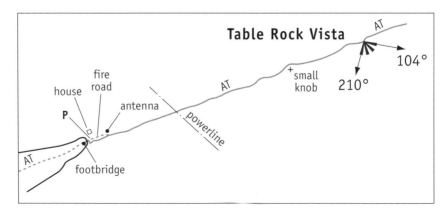

at you. The first is the antenna array on Second Mountain 3 miles away on your right, and the second is the power-line cut over the same ridge, with one huge tower silhouetted against the sky. These make sweeping landscape photos difficult. The best images from here are of a delightful white barn at 104° tucked in the valley below, preferably shot with a long lens.

During my night trek in for sunrise, I heard two great horned owls hooting to each other for much of the trip. Near sunrise, a pileated woodpecker's call shattered the morning calm, followed by a growing chorus of smaller birds. I love listening to the waking world at dawn.

Hike 64 Weiser Hang Glider Launch Site, Weiser State Forest (Haldeman Tract)

Type: ridge	**Height:** 1,656 feet
Rating: 5	**Best times:** afternoon through sunset
GPS: 40° 31.123'N, 76° 46.740'W	**Difficulty:** easy
Faces. 282'	**Distance:** .25 mile
Field of view: 244° to 320°	**Time:** 10 minutes
Relief: 10 feet	**Elevation change:** 55 feet
Elevation difference: 1,130 feet	**Best lenses:** 35mm to 100mm

Directions: Some of the Weiser State Forest road signs are missing, so keep an eye on your odometer. From the intersection of US 209 and PA 225 in the town of Elizabethville, take PA 225 south for 1 mile. Turn left onto Quarry Road (T 587) and follow it for 1 mile to the intersection with Mountain House Road (SR 1003). At this merge, the road becomes White Oak Road (T 585). Follow the twisting White Oak Road, and cross into state forest lands in 1.1 miles. The road curves sharply to the right and begins climbing. At 2.8 miles, Dietrich Road comes in from the left. White Oak makes a long, looping right and intersects with Wolf Pond Road .7 mile after Dietrich. Turn right onto Wolf Pond and follow for 2.4 miles to the parking area. GPS coordinates: 40° 31.021'N, 76° 46.684'W

If you're not into mountain hiking or ridge running, then this is the one place you need to see. This west-facing vista view is the best sunset location in the region. From the parking area, walk north along a grassy road for 150 yards, and follow an opening through the large meadow to your left. The launch site is a wide gap in the trees. A large and imposing warning sign informs fliers of the many licensing requirements, along with the need to inform range control at Fort Indiantown Gap when they fly, which strikes me as odd.

This brief walk brings you to a splendid view of Wyenisco Valley. Your position is atop the western flank of Broad Mountain, framed by two adjacent ridges. Wyenisco Valley is dotted with handsome farms, and their numerous

Twilight on the Valley. On a humid weekend in May, haze dulled the texture of the sunlight on the trees filling the valley below. I waited for the sun to set over the ridge on the right, when the warm sky glow illuminated the valley evenly. *Canon EOS Digital Rebel, Tokina 20–35, polarizer, 2-stop graduate, ISO200 setting, f/16 @ .5 sec.*

silos punctuate the scene. A regrowing clear-cut sits below you, but it isn't a problem in afternoon light, when it lies in the shadows. To your right are the undulating humps of Berry Mountain, and to the extreme right are Mahatango Mountain and finally the large ridge of Shade Mountain some 35 miles distant. On the near left, Dividing Ridge peters out about 6 miles away, and farther left, extending as far as you can see, is the crest of Peters Mountain. Although you can't see the Susquehanna River, it lies 6 miles ahead, and its course can be traced by following the mountain gaps north.

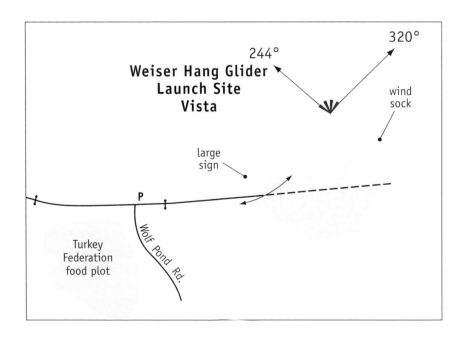

Hike 65 Wyalusing Rocks, Bradford County

Type: cliff	Height: 1,175 feet
Rating: 4+	Best times: midmorning through sunset
GPS: 41° 41.448'N, 76° 16.372'W	Difficulty: easy
Faces: 280°	Distance: 50 yards
Field of view: 220° to 340°	Time: 10 minutes
Relief: 100 feet	Elevation change: 10 feet
Elevation difference: 539 feet	Best lenses: 35mm to 125mm

Directions: From the US 220/US 6 interchange just south of Towanda, take Business Route US 220/US 6 into town. Turn right on US 6 east, crossing the Susquehanna River, and follow for 13.3 miles to a large parking area on the right. GPS coordinates: 41° 41.513'N, 76° 16.383'W

Topographic maps indicate Wyalusing Rocks to be about .2 mile farther up the road. That's because this cliff formation runs for perhaps .4 mile. The best exposures, however, are here at the signed overlook. The main overlook is a large fenced area looking northwest. To the right, fouling a nice farm scene, is a huge equipment shed with many school buses parked nearby. I don't recommend shooting from this position.

Instead, find the grass path at the parking lot's end and follow it to a series of three rock exposures. All three cliffs are undercut and have no foreground obstructions. They also allow you to face up- and downriver, thus eliminating the pole shed from view. The only issue is a hilltop house or building along 299° several miles away, which is oriented perfectly to reflect midday sun like a mirror. I had to wait nearly half an hour for this intense spot to disappear before I could make record shots of the overlook. When photographing the river, I recommend shooting verticals. The path ends at the last cliff.

It is unfortunate that the cliffs were recently marked with white graffiti. As a result, it's no longer possible to use the rocks as an anchoring fore-

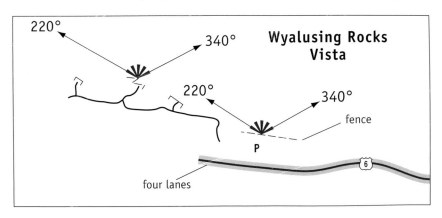

Skiff in River. As this small boat wove its way up the Susquehanna, it left a curved wake. This added a hint of visual interest to the river's mirrored surface. *Canon EOS Digital Rebel, Tokina 20–35, polarizer, 81A warming filter, 2-stop graduate, ISO100 setting, f/8 @ 1.3 sec.*

ground. You must set your tripod right at the precipice to keep the graffiti out of the frame.

You may have maps or brochures indicating that there is an overlook called French Azylium 10 miles from Towanda. When I surveyed it, the entire overlook was overgrown with large trees. A restaurant was being refurbished, however, so perhaps the view has been cleaned up. It's worth a stop. Look for a pair of medieval-looking parapets hidden behind three buildings on the west side of US 6.

Hike 66 Trout Run, Appalachian Trail, SGL-211

Type: cobble	**Height:** 1,369 feet
Rating: 3	**Best times:** early morning through late afternoon
GPS: 40° 28.921'N, 76° 35.644'W	**Difficulty:** moderate
Faces: 143°	**Distance:** 7.6 miles
Field of view: 94° to 200°	**Time:** 3 hours, 45 minutes
Relief: 15 feet	**Elevation change:** 1,440 feet
Elevation difference: 764 feet	**Best lenses:** 50mm to 125mm

Directions: From the I-81/US 209 interchange near Tower City, take US 209 south into Tower City. Turn left on PA 305 south and follow for 1.5 miles. Turn left onto Goldmine Road (SR 3015) and follow for 7 miles as it switchbacks up and over Second Mountain. Just before the intersection with PA 443, turn right onto Greenpoint School Road and proceed 1.5 miles to a wide spot on the left where the Appalachian Trail exits a small grove of tress from the right. GPS coordinates: 40° 29.404'N, 76° 33.105'W

What I both enjoyed and disliked about this trail was navigating the pink-blazed side trail to the view. Because it's not its mandate, the Pennsylvania Game Commission does not perform trail maintenance on state game lands. That job falls to an army of volunteers who love the Appalachian Trail (AT), and they do a very good job. It's just that this side trail has sort of fallen off the maintenance radar and can be a bit difficult to follow, which can be fun or frustrating, depending on your viewpoint. But no matter, what's life without the occasional challenge?

From the parking area, cross the road to follow the white-blazed AT. It begins as a pleasant farmland stroll, entering the trees at Second Mountain's base in .33 mile. You are now on state game lands. Here the trail remains level, meandering through quiet open woodland. At .68 mile, the AT turns right and begins a vigorous climb all the way to a false summit at .9 mile. All you've done is climbed a bench heading an unnamed gap. At this false top, the trail descends perhaps 40 feet, then is level for the next quarter mile, making for a delightful walk—that is, until the next turn uphill.

At 1.3 miles, the final climb begins. There's a double blaze marking a right turn, and the old AT route ahead is blocked by small trees, but in the dark it would be easy to miss this turn. After a series of short switchbacks, the AT makes a sweeping left as it crests the mountain to head more or less southwest. From here to the next trail intersection, the AT is straight and fairly level.

A narrow pipeline right-of-way is at 2.1 miles. This pipeline is fairly old and looks more like a woods road. At 2.3 miles, you come to a woods road at an X-shaped intersection. Look for a fire ring a dozen yards to your left. Here the trail to the vista bears left and stays on the high ground, while the

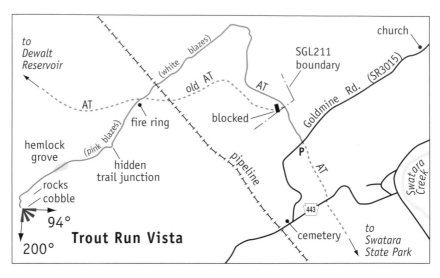

white-blazed AT bears right and descends (a hard left takes you down to Ridge Road a mile west of the parking area). There are no visible blazes marking the view trail here, only the fire ring and an oddly placed boulder that's turned on edge, acting as a cairn of sorts.

Bear left around the fire ring and look for the first of an intermittent series of dark pink blazes. This side trail starts out as an easy-to-follow woods road, then quickly closes in to become a footpath. The best indicator to use if you're hiking in the dark is to look for trodden-down leaf litter. After leveling for a bit, the pink-blazed trail curves left and begins to climb near 2.5 miles. As the trail tops out at 2.8 miles, it turns right. Take care at this point, as there is another indistinct footpath heading straight. Faded pink blazes appear just before and after this turn. Keep a sharp eye out. After the turn, look for a large stone outcrop on your left.

Near 3 miles, the trail passes through a tight little hemlock grove, then meanders left and right, making it difficult to find blazes. Many trees bearing blazes have fallen, so you need to look on the ground or for large chunks of bark with pink on them. Also, a number of blowdowns make progress slow going. Strangely enough, a large cairn is found at 3.3 miles. Shortly after, turn left and pass through a large fernery, then right once again. At 3.6 miles, the trail makes a hard left at a well-marked double pink blaze. This is the only marked turn on the whole trail. Passing through another carpet of ferns, the trail descends toward a bright gap as traffic noise begins to filter to you, and finally at 3.7 miles, it descends to the mountain flank cobble.

As with most cobbles, where you stand determines the view. From the cobble's extreme right, you can get a long-lens shot of Swatara Gap, and from the left, there's a similar shot of Indiantown Gap. PA 443 is not visible but is the source of the traffic noise you hear. The houses you see are all about 1 mile away and sit along Ridge Road. At a bearing of 178° is a large home sitting on the flank of Blue Mountain. They must have a heck of a view.

Hike 67 **Kimmel View and Fisher Lookout, Appalachian Trail**

Kimmel View

Type: ledge	Field of view: 120° to 244°
Rating: 5	Relief: 30 feet
GPS: 40° 30.662'N, 76° 20.667'W	Elevation difference: 895 feet
Faces: 160°	Height: 1,343 feet

Fisher Lookout

Type: ledge	Field of view: 120° to 228°
Rating: 3	Relief: 20 feet
GPS: 40° 30.608'N, 76° 21.418'W	Elevation difference: /94 feet
Faces: 160°	Height: 1,304 feet
Best times: sunrise through early midmorning	Time: 1 hour
Difficulty: easy	Elevation change: 268 feet
Distance: 1.6 miles	Best lenses: 17mm to 250mm

Directions: From I-78 in Bethel, take the PA 501 exit and head north for 5.4 miles to where the Appalachian Trail crosses at a large parking area on the right. GPS coordinates: 40° 30.769'N, /6° 20.666'W

Looking out upon Great Valley from the southernmost ridge of the Appalachian Range, you can see mile after mile of handsome farms. This short hike is what you might call "low-hanging fruit" in marketing lingo. Both views are easy to get to, even in snow cover. From the large parking area, cross PA 501 and follow the white-blazed Appalachian Trail (AT) west (southbound). The trail descends and makes a sharp turn at Kimmel View, which you reach in only .15 mile. Of the two views, Kimmel is by far the better.

Like many AT vista points, this ledge is a series of tilted rock slabs that have distinct tiers, and any one of them makes a nice shooting perch. The only issue is that in morning light, rocks to your right are sunlit while those on the left remain in shadow. Also, any moisture on the rocks acts like a mirror during sunrise. To your right, a small side trail leads about 20 yards to another, smaller perch. When I shot a wintry sunrise, the gentle moo of dairy cows wafted to me on the still, crisp air.

Continue along the AT, and in about 100 yards you come to a hang glider launch site, which is just a wide opening in the trees. Note the wind sock on the right. I haven't rated this view, as I don't think it's worth the effort to try to shoot, although it is a nice picnic spot. From here rocks come and go as the trail gently rises and falls. This is some easy AT hiking, and you're always within earshot of PA 501 in case something should go wrong.

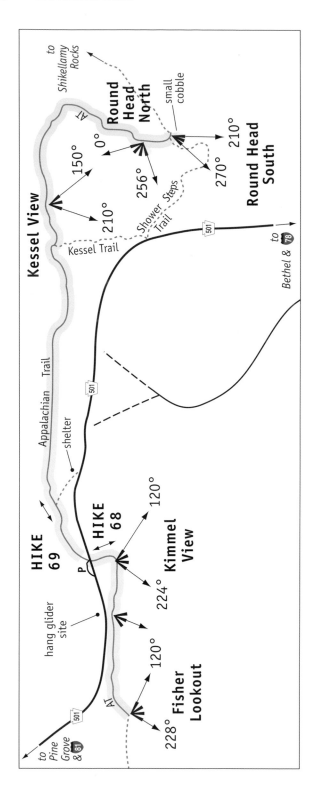

New Snow at Dawn. Fresh snow is the perfect time to get out and shoot, and with this view so close to the road, there's no excuse not to venture out. A small patch of green lens flare was removed using Photoshop. *Canon EOS Digital Rebel, Tokina 20–35, polarizer, 10CC magenta, 2-stop graduate, ISO100 setting, f/16 @ .5 sec.*

At .8 mile, you arrive at Fisher Lookout, which honors Bob Fisher for his fifty years of service to the Blue Mountain Eagle Climbing Club. The view is similar to Kimmel, but here brush clogs the foreground, making this only a long-lens shot.

Hike 68 Round Head, Appalachian Trail

Kessel View

Type: cobble	**Field of view:** 153° to 210°
Rating: 2	**Relief:** 5 feet
GPS: 40° 30.915'N, 76° 18.917'W	**Elevation difference:** 998 feet
Faces: south to southwest	**Height:** 1,405 feet

Round Head North

Type: ledge	**Field of view:** 256° to 000°
Rating: 4	**Relief:** 20 feet
GPS: 40° 30.567'N, 76° 18.600'W	**Elevation difference:** 1,131 feet
Faces: south to southwest	**Height:** 1,510 feet

Round Head South

Type: ledge	**Field of view:** 210° to 246°
Rating: 3	**Relief:** 20 feet
GPS: 40° 30.450'N, 76° 18.583'W	**Elevation difference:** 794 feet
Faces: south to southwest	**Height:** 1,099 feet
Best times: late afternoon through sunset	**Time:** 2 hours, 30 minutes
Difficulty: moderate	**Elevation change:** 282 feet
Distance: 5.5 miles	**Best lenses:** 28mm to 200mm

Directions: From I-78 in Bethel, take the PA 501 exit and head north for 5.4 miles to where the Appalachian Trail crosses at a large parking area on the right. GPS coordinates: 40° 30.769'N, 76° 20.666'W

The Appalachian Trail (AT) crosses just down the road, so it's much safer to walk from the parking area along a wide trail that passes a large blue trash can, which in turn crosses a blue-blazed trail in about 50 feet. Turn right onto the blue-blazed trail and in about another 50 feet you come to the white-blazed AT. Turn left onto the AT to head east (northbound). There are number of intersecting woods roads, some heavily used by local farmers and some long abandoned, so always look for white blazes ahead and behind to make sure you don't inadvertently walk off the trail. Cross the first road at .13 mile and the second at .25 mile. At .4 mile, you come to a blue-blazed trail crossing (left goes to the Applebee campsite and right to Pilger Run Spring). Continue ahead on the white-blazed AT.

From here, the trail alternates between typical AT rocky and a leaf-covered dirt footpath. After a very shallow descent near .5 mile, the AT rises and then drops again at .6 mile before leveling again around 1 mile. Here the unique scent of large dairy farms is rather intense. At 1.8 miles, a blue-blazed trail drops from the ridge on your right. This is the head of the Kessel Trail, which cuts a straight line from here to the base of Round Head before climbing back up on Showers Steps. Continuing along the AT, in about 100 yards more you arrive at a moderate-size hillside cobble. This is Kessel View.

Kessel View is actually a narrow alley through the trees and provides a nice view of Round Head's western flank. In the distance are several farms and a large turkey house at 199°, which is the large shed with the shiny metal roof you see about 1.6 miles out in the valley. Closer in, just beyond the nearest line of trees, is a well-kept red bank barn. This makes a nice long-lens shot.

After Kessel View, the AT makes a long, rocky climb to get to the top of Round Head. After the AT tops out, you'll come to another moderate-size cobble that is Round Head's north vista, arriving at 2.65 miles. Facing west, you look along the flank of Blue Mountain and can easily see Kessel View.

Where you stand determines the field of view. Farther to the right, your view is to the west, and from a left position, it is northwest.

Through the notch where PA 501 crosses, you have a really fine view of Second and Sharp Mountains, which lie about 10 miles away. What makes this view perfect for sunsets, particularly in autumn, is the miniature valley to your right formed by Little and Blue Mountains. I watched a bright orange and black antique Stearman biplane flying back and forth through the ridge gap at Meckville and wished I had brought my 400mm lens. The only issue for real wide-angle work is three microwave towers lying at 300° and 288°. The one at 288° is small and will show up only when silhouetted against a bright sky, so take care.

Now I tend to notice odd things when I hike, probably because while I'm jotting notes in my journal, I am very quiet, allowing the woods to come alive around me. So here I was, jotting away, when a black vulture landed in a tree near me. Vultures aren't as skittish as other raptors, and they'll stay put unless really pressed, so it's quite common to see them in trees or on ridgetops sunning themselves. After writing some, I noticed this bird hadn't extended its wings to sun itself. It was kind of bent forward and looked for all the world as if it were flashing me a moon. Rhythmically, it would lean forward, tail rising toward me, and splay open its tail feathers like a turkey. After watching this several times, I noticed that the little feathers around its anus were opening and closing (yes, I have no life).

After a few more of these heaves, the ungainly black bird turned its featherless head my way, looking at me with one black beady eye. Its posture and body motion looked for all the world as if it were pleading with me as if to say, "Dude, a little privacy please." It was a comical moment, so I left my carrion-eating companion, hoping that nature would help it expel whatever its violent contortions couldn't.

If you continue along the AT, you'll arrive at Round Head's south vista at the top of Showers Steps. The view here faces southwest and is so-so. If you'd like to continue on to Shikellamy Overlook, follow the AT another 2.5 miles.

Hike 69 The Pinnacle and Pulpit Rock, Hamburg

The Pinnacle

Type: ledge	**Field of view:** 40° to 170°
Rating: 5	**Relief:** 50 feet
GPS: 40° 36.800′N, 75° 54.733′W	**Elevation difference:** 1,153 feet
Faces: 100°	**Height:** 1,563 feet

Pulpit Rock

Type: ledge	**Field of view:** 26° to 100°
Rating: 5	**Relief:** 20 feet
GPS: 40° 35.801'N, 75° 55.883'W	**Elevation difference:** 1,016 feet
Faces: 110°	**Height:** 1,499 feet
Best times: sunrise through late afternoon	**Trail:** Pulpit Rock
Distance: 9.4 miles for both views	**Distance:** 3.25 miles
Difficulty: moderate to difficult	**Difficulty:** moderate to difficult
Time: 5 hours	**Time:** 3 hours
Trail: The Pinnacle	**Elevation change:** 1,800 feet for both views
Distance: 8 miles	The Pinnacle 1,500 feet
Difficulty: moderate	Pulpit Rock 800 feet
Time: 4 hours, 30 minutes	**Best lenses:** 17mm to 400mm

Directions: From the PA Turnpike Northeast Extension (I-476) interchange at I-78/US 22, take I-78/US 22 west for 17.7 miles, and exit for PA 143 (Lenhartsville). At the bottom of the ramp, turn right onto PA 143 south, passing under I-78, and drive .4 mile to a T intersection. Turn right onto Old US 22 (SR 4028) and proceed 3.1 miles to Reservoir Road, where a small church is on the left and a farmhouse on the right obscures the turn. Turn right, pass under I-78, and follow Reservoir Road to a dead-end parking area in 1 mile. GPS coordinates: 40° 34.983'N, 75° 56.517'W

The Pinnacle and Pulpit Trail is the state's best-known vista loop hike. Its proximity to Philadelphia means that on any nice weekend, both views can be mobbed, which is why you should get to them before dawn. The Pinnacle and Pulpit Loop is a straightforward hike, which I've divided into two in-and-out hikes so that you can budget your time.

The Pinnacle

The Pinnacle is an 8-mile round-trip. At the reservoir trailhead is a large billboard-size map that shows all the trails on the ridge. Walk past the big map on the gravel road. Follow this road around a bend and across a road bridge at about .5 mile. From this bridge, the white-blazed AT proceeds straight ahead into the woods. Instead, turn left and proceed uphill on the road to an intersection at .75 mile. The road straight ahead takes you to the Pinnacle (Pulpit Rock is to the right). Go straight uphill, passing the Hamburg Reservoir on your left. Continue steeply uphill to a large grassy area at 2.25 miles. This is the helipad noted on the parking area map. Turn right onto the white-blazed AT, and follow it to 3.8 miles and the Pinnacle, which is well signed and marked by a 10-foot-tall stone cairn. This very long cliff affords a nearly 180-degree field of view. At the very point, you can get a nice shot of the stone New Bethel Church in the valley below.

3 Days after 9/11. When shooting afternoon light, you need to arrive a couple hours before sunset, since shadows will darken the valley below about an hour before sunset, rendering it as a large black patch on film. *Canon EOS Rebel Xs, Tokina 20–35, 2-stop graduate, Kodak E100VS, f/27 @ 2 sec.*

I've been to the Pinnacle and Pulpit Rock many times. One particular sunny Friday afternoon, I simply had to get away from the news. You see, it was September 14, 2001, and I needed to escape for a few hours. When I got to the Pinnacle, it was eerily calm. There were no low-flying planes on approach into nearby Allentown, nor were there any contrails in the afternoon sky. I wrote about what I was feeling in an AT trail log, and then shouted at the wind for a few moments before settling down to the business of photographing the farms below.

My hike back in the dark held a surprise. About a mile from the helipad, something passed through my headlamp beam and startled me, like a flashbulb going off. Then it happened again. It took a few moments for me to realize that a bat was circling my head, at eye level, and coming ever closer to my face. Every twenty seconds or so, it would pass in front of me and try to grab insects hovering near my face. I became fascinated by it.

Now many of you are probably skeeving over the idea of a bat flitting around your head. But to me, such encounters should be savored and enjoyed. Between my sweat and headlamp beam, I was providing my little brown companion with a movable feast. And it was providing me with insight into bat feeding behavior and flight characteristics. It seemed like a fair trade.

The bat kept me company for another mile, until the trail closed in and it couldn't easily circle. I saw the little guy zip down the trail away from me, turn around, and come headlong at me, which it did a few times. I guess it didn't like the increased effort involved in getting dinner, however, and soon it departed.

Then a thought came to me: Here was a bat doing what bats do despite what had happened on that horrible Tuesday morning. My nocturnal friend had given me a small gift. He reminded me that life goes on.

Pulpit Rock

Pulpit Rock can be reached by a 3.25-mile round-trip up a well-groomed fire road with a harsh 800-foot elevation gain.

From the intersection at .75 mile mentioned in the directions to the Pinnacle, turn right and proceed steeply uphill until you come to an astronomical observatory at 1.6 miles. Near the largest dome is a small, white signpost, and beyond it is a trail near a pit toilet. Follow this trail about 20 yards and you're at Pulpit Rock, a smallish rocky outcropping with a wonderful panorama.

Sitting atop Pulpit Rock in a foot of snow, facing a February sunrise, I gazed upon the world 900 feet below, blanketed by fresh snow and looking like a Currier and Ives greeting card. I couldn't help but feel sorry for the people sleeping in their homes and farms below. They were missing the greatest show Mother Nature puts on, the magical light of dawn the day after a major snowstorm. You too can experience this little bit of nature's majesty—that is, if you set the alarm for 2 A.M.

Loop Hike

To complete an 8.5-mile loop hike, exit either viewpoint using the white-blazed AT. To get from Pulpit Rock to the Pinnacle, walk away from the vista keeping the large cairn on your right. You'll arrive at Pulpit Rock at 7 miles. To get from Pulpit Rock to the Pinnacle, exit Pulpit Rock keeping the view on

Summer Solstice Dawn. Being on the rail at 3 A.M. is all you need to do in order to get a shot like this. *Canon EOS Rebel Xs, Tokina 20–35, 2-stop graduate, 81A warming filter, Kodak E100VS, f/27 @ 4 sec.*

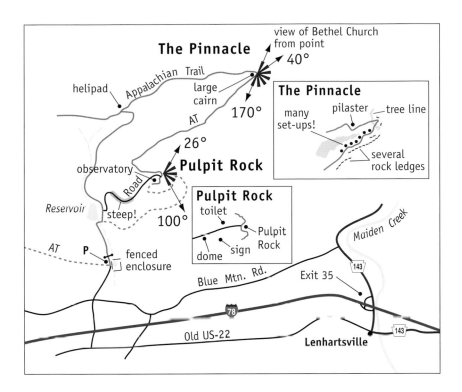

your right. Follow the white-blazed and well-trodden AT to the Pinnacle, arriving at 4.7 miles. The AT between the views is also known as the Valley Rim Trail, and it can get quite rocky. In fact, for about a mile, you can rock-hop such that your feet don't touch soil. I consider this sort of thing fun. You might not.

Hike 70 Hawk Mountain, Berks County

South Lookout

Type: ledge	Field of view: 26° to 100°
Rating: 4	Relief: 20 feet
GPS: 40° 38.174'N, 75° 59.140'W	Elevation difference: 650 feet
Faces: 60°	Height: 1,405 feet

North Lookout

Type: cobble	Field of view: 300° to 140°
Rating: 5	Relief: 10 feet
GPS: 40° 38.505'N, 75° 59.472'W	Elevation difference: 900 feet
Faces: 100°	Height: 1,522 feet

Sunset Rocks	
Type: cobble	**Field of view:** 240° to 340°
Rating: 2	**Relief:** 10 feet
GPS: 40° 38.482′N, 75° 59.685′W	**Elevation difference:** 800 feet
Faces: 290°	**Height:** 1,460 feet
East Rocks	
Type: ledge	**Field of view:** 120° to 220°
Rating: 4	**Relief:** 15 feet
GPS: 40° 38.692′N, 75° 58.896′W	**Elevation difference:** 450 feet
Faces: 180°	**Height:** 1,444 feet
Best times: midmorning through late afternoon	**Time:** 4 hours
Difficulty: moderate	**Elevation change:** 240 feet
Distance: 2.5 miles	**Best lenses:** 20mm to 300mm

Directions: From the I-78/PA 61 interchange at Port Clinton, take PA 61 north for 4.5 miles to the traffic light at PA 895 in the village of Molino. Turn right onto PA 895 north and follow it for 2.5 miles to intersection with Hawk Mountain Road in the village of Drehersville. Turn right onto Hawk Mountain Road, cross the Little Schuylkill River, and climb the steep ridge to the visitor center on the right in 2 miles. GPS coordinates: 40° 38.083′N, 75° 59.217′W

No location in Pennsylvania offers such easy foot access to as many wonderful views as Hawk Mountain does. It's often crowded on fall weekends during the raptor migration, but spring weekends offer the opportunity to experience true solitude from all the lookouts. Because access is so easy, I strongly recommend you try to get here after a snowstorm. That's when the landscape is magical from North Lookout. Perhaps the best thing Hawk Mountain has going for it is that during the migration it caters to kids with different programs ranging from live raptor shows to coloring books. This is the perfect place to expose youngsters to the great outdoors of Penn's Woods. Hawk Mountain's work to protect raptors and their migration routes extends far beyond the sanctuary property atop Blue Mountain. In fact, it goes all the way to Argentina. Please make a donation in addition to the admission fee to support the efforts. It'll be put to great use.

If you're curious what the views from Hawk Mountain are like, check out the virtual tour on its website, hawkmountain.org. It's a lot of fun. Also, check the website or call ahead to verify their hours of operation.

The easiest vista to get to is South Lookout, which is about 200 yards from the parking area. The view from here looks into a bowl created by a massive ridge offset, common in the Ridge and Valley Province. Imagine laying a cloth napkin on a table and pushing evenly across two sides to create soft folds in the fabric, then grabbing the other two sides to sheer the folds.

Moonset Through Earth Shadow. Twice a month, moonset occurs near sunrise. Although this might seem like a lucky shot, it's not. It's what happens when planning and experience coincide. *Canon EOS Rebel Xs, Tokina 20–35, 2-stop graduate, 10CC Magenta, Kodak E100VS, f/27 @ 8 sec.*

The swirl pattern created is what the topography between the Pinnacle (Hike 69) and Hawk Mountain looks like from the air.

North Lookout has the best view in the sanctuary and is reached by passing South Lookout on the Lookout Trail. Hike .5 mile from the entrance gate to a side trail called the Express Trail, which climbs a steep shortcut to Kettle View and then North Lookout .7 mile from the gate. On the way to North Lookout, you'll pass by four other viewpoints, all of which are signed and have nice views.

North Lookout is a ridgetop cobble covering about 2 acres, and it affords a panoramic view. To the north and west, you can see the steam plume from Berwick's nuclear generating station. To the east, the crest of Blue Mountain extends into the distance. To your right, you can see the boulder fields along the River of Rocks Trail. To the far right, the promontory marking the limit of your horizon view is the Pinnacle along the famed Appalachian Trail. The valley in the distance is Great Valley, also known as Lehigh Valley, which extends from central Virginia to New Jersey. Don't stay put when you shoot from here. By simply moving around, you change your perspective of the landscape considerably.

This boulder field was created by freeze-thaw cycles along the glacial margin during the last ice age some ten thousand years ago. The Wisconsin Ice Sheet stopped about 40 miles north, near what is now Hickory Run State Park, so the climate here was more like the arctic tundra of today. It's inter-

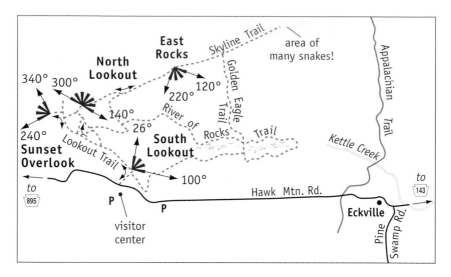

esting to think that ten thousand years ago, you would have been able to see mammoths wandering through the valley below.

To reach Sunset Rocks, you take the Lookout Trail. Rather than turning on the Express Trail, continue straight another 100 yards, passing the stairway to North Lookout. At the next intersection, turn left to get to Sunset Rocks. You'll need to navigate through and over some boulders, which make getting here a bit more demanding than North Lookout.

Sunset Rocks is a small cobble with larger trees standing close in. Here the view is to the west and looks down on new development along PA 895. When I first shot here in 2000, there were no homes, but by 2002, large homes began to sprout from the surrounding farmland like weeds. Now the view is all but spoiled by development.

Getting to East Rocks is, to say the least, a challenge. You have two choices. The first is to descend the River of Rocks Trail from where it connects with the Lookout Trail near the Express Trail. The descent is steep and quite rocky. After .3 mile, turn left at the intersection with Golden Eagle Trail to climb back up the ridge. Once on the ridgetop, which you reach at .6 mile, turn right and take the difficult-to-follow Skyline Trail to East Rocks at 1.3 miles. A more direct route is to follow the blue-blazed Skyline Trail straight off the end of North Lookout. The descent off the lookout's nose is a hand-over-hand 20-foot rock scramble, after which you reach East Rocks in .6 mile.

East Rocks is tucked into the trees lining the ridge and has a unique view. It's also extraordinarily quiet. Though North Lookout can be mobbed during the migration's peak in October, East Rocks rarely has more than two or three people, even during the most crowded weekends. This vista looks into the ridge offset's bowl like South Lookout does, but because you're almost a mile downridge facing more south, the view into Great Valley is more extensive than even from North Lookout. You also get good look at the Pinnacle's north side.

Hike 71 **Bake Oven Knob, Lehigh County**

Type: ledge	**Best times:** sunrise through midmorning
Rating: 5	**Difficulty:** easy; stairway climb through rocks
GPS: 40° 44.922'N, 75° 44.029'W	**Distance:** .4 mile
Faces: 110°	**Time:** 30 minutes
Field of view: 80° to 160°	**Elevation change:** 100 feet
Relief: 30 feet	**Best lenses:** 17mm to 100mm
Height: 1,000 feet	

Directions: From the Mahoning Valley interchange on the PA Turnpike Northeast Extension (I-476), exit for Jim Thorpe. At the bottom of the ramp, turn right onto US 209 south for Jim Thorpe and Weissport. After 1.7 miles, turn left at a traffic light onto PA 248 south. Follow for 3 miles, and exit for PA 895 at Bowmanstown. Follow PA 895 west for 4.6 miles, and turn left onto Sand Quarry/Germans Road for the village of Germans. This turn is shortly after passing a power line and electrical substation on the left. In .4 mile, after crossing Lizzard Creek, bear right onto Germans Road. In .7 mile, turn left onto Bake Oven Road and make the switchback climb to a large parking area on the left in 1.7 miles. GPS coordinates: 40° 44.668'N, 75° 44.288'W

One warm August evening, I brought my wife and a friend to this famous vista to see the closest approach of Mars to our own planet in the last sixty-five thousand years. There was a thick haze layer on the horizon, yet

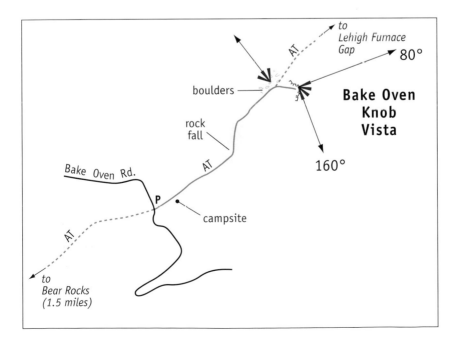

God Beams. Haze on the horizon made shooting sunrise a bust. Just as I was about to head back, the sun breached the haze layer, and a fan of "God beams" reached through the sky. Made with a borrowed medium-format camera, this shot is what convinced me to buy my own large-format rig. *Mamiya RZ-67 Pro, 50mm Schneider Superangulaon f/4.5, 6x7 220 roll film back, Fuji Velvia, f/32 @ 5 sec.*

viewing conditions for the conjunction of Mars were still good. With a selection of cheeses, crackers, and bottles of white and red wine set out on a checkered tablecloth, we settled in to watch the planet rise. This once-in-an-age event did not disappoint. After Mars was above the haze, it was bright and clearly visible to the naked eye, a spectacular sight indeed. This terrific location and ease of getting to it are what make this mountain vista a must-see.

The trail to Bake Oven Knob is easy, and it's a fine place to bring kids. During the fall raptor migration, it makes for a good location to watch this annual spectacle, and Hawk Mountain Sanctuary has observers here.

From the enormous parking area, head east (northbound) along the white-blazed Appalachian Trail (AT). The AT exits from a corner of the lot, so do not cross the road. The wide trail is level for the first 100 yards and then begins a slow climb, becoming ever more rocky until you encounter the knob's boulder-filled west side. Here a set of stone-slab stairs climbs through the rockfall. At the top, you'll see the foundation of an old observation tower. To your left is a north-facing vista, and off toward your right is the ledge of Bake Oven Knob. Bear right and walk the last 30 yards through large rocks to the vista point.

Bake Oven Knob faces a little south of east, making it the perfect location for shooting sunrise from mid-October to early May. It's perfect for the equinoxes and winter solstice. Closer to the summer solstice, the sun rises over the ridge of Blue Mountain to your left. Normally I like to use rock ledges to form an image's foreground. That's not possible here because of the extensive graffiti, so you'll need to set up close to the edge. The site also has some other problems. Radio tower lights in the vicinity of Allentown 16.7 miles away make shooting twilight difficult. More towers 5.4 miles away to the west of Lehigh Gap restrict the ability to shoot panoramas. And a sand mine immediately below makes shooting the facing ridge difficult. The best shots are of cloudscapes, atmospherics, and landscapes to your southeast. If you want to attempt winter landscapes, approach the knob from the south, as that road gets more sun and is wider than the north approach. There is no winter maintenance, so plan accordingly.

If you're up for some exploring, a small view called Bear Rocks sits 1.4 miles west of the parking area along the AT, and the famous Knife's Edge is just another .5 mile farther on. Both are fun to crawl around on, but they aren't very good for photography.

Hike 72 Lehigh Gorge West Side, State Game Lands 141, Carbon County

Hinckley Rocks

Type: cliff	**Field of view:** 86° to 205°
Rating: 4	**Relief:** 100 feet
GPS: 40° 53.879′N, 75° 45.500′W	**Elevation difference:** 931 feet
Faces: 146°	**Height:** 1,525 feet

Vista 2

Type: ledge	**Field of view:** 75° to 169°
Rating: 4	**Relief:** 10 feet
GPS: 40° 54.498′N, 75° 45.163′W	**Elevation difference:** 708 feet
Faces: 128°	**Height:** 1,384 feet
Best times: midmorning through late afternoon	**Time:** 3 hours, 30 minutes
Difficulty: strenuous to head of Onoko Run, easy on ridgetop	**Elevation change:** 1,100 feet
Distance: 5.8 miles	**Best lenses:** 35mm to 200mm

Directions: From the PA Turnpike (I-476) interchange at Lehighton, take US 209 south for 2 miles toward Lehighton and Jim Thorpe. After crossing over the Lehigh River, turn right and continue on US 209 south for 4.3 miles, passing through the historic district of Jim Thorpe, to the traffic light with PA 903. Turn right onto PA 903 and cross over the Lehigh River again. Once across, PA 903 makes a sharp left, and .2 mile after, it turns right at a stop sign where right-turn traffic keeps moving. A small and nearly invisible sign opposite says Glen Onoko Access. Stop at the stop sign, and then continue straight down a steep hill and turn left into the park. Follow the park road for 1.8 miles to the parking area. GPS coordinates: 40° 53.004′N, 75° 45.617′W

You may not make it to the west-rim vistas overlooking the Lehigh River from this access point. In all honesty, the big reason for the large parking area is the four waterfalls along Onoko Run, which are described in my book *Pennsylvania Waterfalls.* As beautiful as they are, leave the waterfalls for the return trip. After several miles of rim hiking, you'll appreciate the icy shower of Onoko Falls all the more.

Find the concrete stairs next to the Lehigh Gorge State Park map pedestal and picnic table. The trail to the falls and rim begins by descending these stairs. Please read the Game Commission sign at the bottom, and I quote: "Hike at your own risk. Sections of this trail are steep and treacherous." This

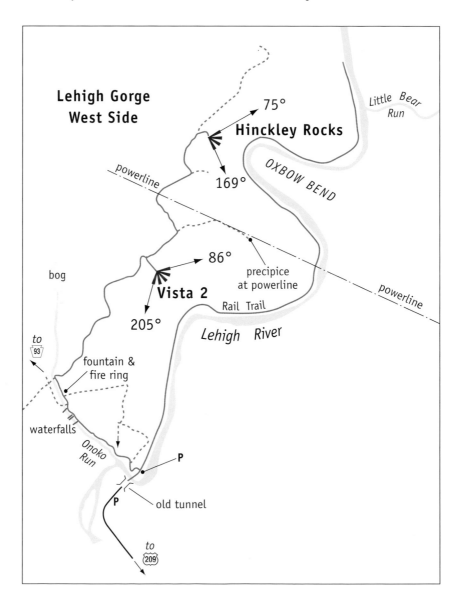

emphatic warning is here because several people have fallen to their death over the years, how many I don't know. Furthermore, Onoko Falls and the rim hike are not in Lehigh Gorge State Park but in State Game Lands 141, and very little trail maintenance is performed by the Game Commission. In fact, several portions of the trail have been washed away over the years. So take your time, and always be aware of your footing.

At the base of the stairs, turn right and pass beneath two railroad bridges, then turn right again, away from the river, and walk parallel to the railroad tracks to climb a small embankment straight ahead of you. Stop when you get level with the railroad tracks. At this point, you're directly opposite the parking lot, not more than 100 feet from where you began. Look around for a low stone wall with a wide trail on top that runs away from the railroad tracks. A few faint orange blazes might be found to mark the start of a 1,000-foot climb to the gorge rim. This portion of the trail is in good shape as it climbs steadily away from the Lehigh River to enter Glen Onoko.

When you pass a graffiti-plastered ledge on your right, beautiful Onoko Run comes into view well below to the left. While the trail remains some-what level, the run rises quickly to meet it. From where they join, the trail gets progressively worse, becoming a series of difficult rock scrambles and root climbs while clinging to the left-hand creek bank. Remain on Onoko Run's left-hand side (the side you're on). At no time will you cross the run. Scrambling along trying not to trip forces you to keep looking down, and it's easy to miss seeing how pretty this steep-sided ravine really is.

Continuing along the steep, root-filled creek bank, at .4 mile you'll reach the lower 25-foot cascade of Chameleon Falls. Backtrack several yards downstream and find a route to scramble up the talus slope of the left-hand bank, and then turn upstream to follow the run. In about 50 yards, you come to the base of Onoko Falls. Backtrack from the falls several yards and scramble up this more navigable talus slope to where a series of ledges disappears into the hillside. (Don't try climbing any of the ledges directly; go around them.) Walk carefully along the narrow ledges to where the run exits a rhododendron grove. There may be a guiding orange blaze or two, but don't count on it.

Proceed upstream with the run on your left, picking a way through the claustrophobic rhododendron grove, and in about 70 yards you come to a 15-foot falls called Hidden Sweet, which is .5 mile from the trailhead. At .55 mile, the steep trail levels off as it enters an open grove of scrubby hemlocks and pitch pines. Nearby is an open area, an old Wahnetah Hotel outbuilding foundation, and a fire ring. Keeping the now weakly flowing run on your left, follow a narrow, poorly blazed but well-trodden footpath to where it intersects a fire road at .75 mile. The run will be out of view but audible the entire way.

In winter, Onoko Glen is too dangerous to climb. Winter parking is 2.25 miles to your left, where the wide fire road intersects PA 93 at 40° 53.526'N, 75° 48.378'W, which is 2.4 miles north of the PA 93/US 209 intersection. Turning right on the fire road will take you to Hinckley Rocks. At 1.7 miles, a wide side trail intersects the fire road from your right. Turn right and you'll arrive at Hinckley Rocks in 1.8 miles. Hinckley Rocks is an impressive 100-foot-wide cliff that looks down upon the Lehigh River and at a pyramid-shaped peak on the far side. To your left are power lines crossing the gorge, which limit your shooting. The vista provides a nice view of Packertown. Shots of the river are not easy to get from here, because a wide gray line created by a bike path slices through the frame.

Return to the fire road and turn right. Here the road is surrounded by pitch pines. It's wide, sandy, and has a few rocks thrown in to make setting a brisk pace challenging. At 2.35 miles, you cross the power-line right-of-way you observed from Hinckley Rocks. Continuing on, another road or wide trail enters from your right at 2.8 miles. Turn right and you'll arrive at the second vista in short order.

This promontory differs from Hinckley Rocks in several ways. Rather than a wide cliff, it consists of two stone ledges separated by a free-standing rock pillar. The ledges have enough room for two or three people at most. Because the apex of Oxbow Bend is hidden from view, a wide-angle image will feel incomplete or divided. I recommend working images looking to your right, using a lens that keeps the power lines out of the frame. Views to the left are best shot with a long lens, exploring and playing graphically with the S-curve of Lehigh Gorge as it disappears into the distance.

Hike 73 Tank Hollow, Lehigh Gorge East Side, Game Lands 141, Carbon County

Type: cliff	**Height:** 1,446 feet
Rating: 3	**Best times:** midmorning through sunset
GPS: 40° 56.919′N, 75° 42.009′W	**Difficulty:** easy
Faces: 270°	**Distance:** 3.4 miles
Field of view: 240° to 14°	**Time:** 1 hour, 15 minutes
Relief: 50 feet	**Elevation change:** 250 feet
Elevation difference: 659 feet	**Best lenses:** 35mm to 100mm

Directions: From the PA Turnpike (I-476) interchange at Lehighton, take US 209 south for 2 miles toward Lehighton and Jim Thorpe. After crossing over the Lehigh River, turn right and continue on US 209 south for 4.3 miles, passing through the historic district of Jim Thorpe, to the traffic light with PA 903. Turn right onto PA 903 and cross over the Lehigh River again. Once across, PA 903 makes a sharp left, and .2 mile after, it turns right at a stop sign where right-turn traffic keeps moving. Turn right and follow PA 903 for 8.3 miles. As soon as you pass under a power line, turn left onto Church Road. Follow it for .8 mile to a Y intersection, and bear right onto Behrens Road (T 506). Take Behrens Road for 1 mile, and make the next right into a large game lands parking area. GPS coordinates: 40° 56.512′N, 75° 40.350′W

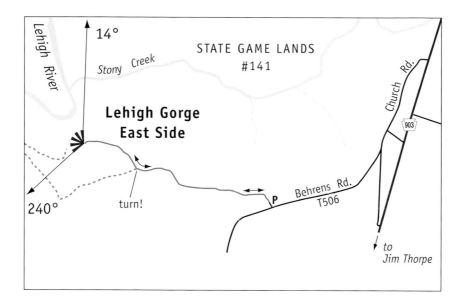

This easy road hike is a good way to expose youngsters to the great out-doors. The game-lands road doubles as a multiuse trail, so expect to see horses and mountain bikers, and always yield to horses by stepping off the road and remaining still.

Walk around the gate and follow the gravel road for .6 mile, passing more parking areas and bearing right at a Y junction. At 1.2 miles, look for a foot-path on the right marked by a 1/2-by-6-inch piece of vinyl nailed to a tree at 40° 56.750′N, 75° 41.544′W. There may be a small cairn nearby as well. Turn right and follow an unblazed but well-worn footpath through pine woods, arriving at a 100-foot-wide cliff at 1.7 miles.

This cliff face is tilted quite a bit and is higher on the south end, the end you entered at, than on the north. Looking straight down into Tank Hollow, the principal view is north up the Lehigh River toward Drakes Creek. The river makes a tight bend as it comes toward you, and it's possible to create a shot with a sweeping U-shape of water. Although the view is wide enough to look southwest over the ridge, confine your images to the river gorge. This also makes a nice summer sunset spot. A juvenile offender boot camp facility is nearby, so don't be surprised if you see groups of kids in orange shirts being force-marched along the gravel roads and trails on this side of the gorge.

Hike 74 Delp Overlook, Appalachian Trail, Carbon County

Type: ledge	**Height:** 1,535 feet
Rating: 5	**Best times:** late afternoon through evening
GPS: 40° 48.733′N, 75° 28.702′W	**Difficulty:** moderate; 300-foot climb through a boulder field
Faces: 186°	**Distance:** 6.7 miles
Field of view: 112° to 260°	**Time:** 2 hours, 45 minutes
Relief: 10 feet	**Elevation change:** 550 feet
Elevation difference: 803 feet	**Best lenses:** 17mm to 200mm

Directions: From the Mahoning Valley interchange on the PA Turnpike Northeast Extension (I-476), exit for Jim Thorpe. At the bottom of the ramp, turn right onto US 209 south for Jim Thorpe and Weissport. After 1.7 miles, turn left at a traffic light onto PA 248 south. Follow for 7 miles, passing the exits for Bowmanstown and Palmerton. As you pass through Lehigh Gap, bear left onto PA 248 for another .4 mile, and then turn left onto Timberline Road. After 2.7 miles, turn left onto PA 946. In 1 mile, turn left onto Blue Mountain Road (SR 4001). Climb the ridge, and after 1.4 miles, look for a parking area on the left before the Appalachian Trail crosses the road. GPS coordinates: 40° 48.358′N, 75° 32.115′W

Delp Overlook is a surprising view. It's rare along this section of Blue Mountain to have cliffs and ledges that don't need to have trees cut back on a regular basis. What I like especially about this view is that it's accessible from three places. From Smith Gap this vista is an 8-mile ridgetop hike, and it's a 4-mile climbing hike via the Delp Trail from a State Game Lands 168 parking area located near the village of Delp.

Exit the rear of the lot and turn right onto an old road grade. Walk north, paralleling the paved highway. After .1 mile, another woods road joins from the left. This is the white-blazed Appalachian Trail (AT). Turn right instead and cross Little Gap Road. From here to .25 mile, the trail passes through a boggy area with rich black soil. In April, look for colorful wildflowers throughout the entire area.

After the bog, the trail begins to climb, easily at first, then rather steeply through a boulder field, until at .5 mile you top out at a gap in the trees with a northwest view. You can also see parts of the "dead zone" on the ridge to the west. This is Weathering Knob, and if you look at the trees in the area, you'll see how beaten up they are. This is due to storms that funnel through the gap. From here, find a wooden antenna platform up the ridge a little way. Now look for a wooden post with white blaze stuck into the boulders on the left. This marks where the AT descends through the boulders. Follow this descending trail and *not* what appears to be a blazed trail working uphill toward the wooden antenna platform.

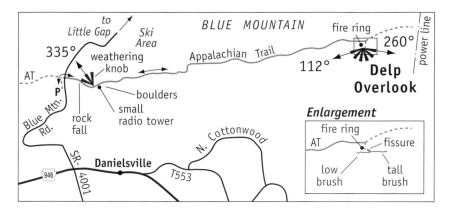

From this point on, the AT meanders left, right, up, and down while finding all the rocks that can be found to slow your way, which is something the AT is famous for. At 3.25 miles, you come to a blue-blazed footpath to the right. This is the side trail to Delp Overlook. Turn right, and you'll quickly come to a large fire ring. Pass the ring to the right, and in about 30 yards, you'll break into the open and arrive at the 50-foot-wide ledge of Delp Overlook.

The view from here is both pastoral and panoramic. In the far distance are several farms with ponds. Fields alternate with woodlands as far as the eye can see. Without a doubt, this is a fantastic picnic location. The best shooting position is adjacent to a cleft in the ledge. Restricting the view east is a cell tower with a white one-second interval strobe at 148°. The best view is along a southwest axis, following a line of low hills that disappear into Great Valley near 250°.

Hike 75 Wolf Rocks, Appalachian Trail, Monroe County

Type: ledge	**Height:** 1,458 feet
Rating: 3	**Best times:** midmorning through sunset
GPS: 40° 55.522'N, 75° 13.282'W	**Difficulty:** easy; woods road and rock hopping
Faces: 322°	**Distance:** 3.8 miles
Field of view: 260° to 25°	**Time:** 2 hours
Relief: 15 feet	**Elevation change:** 200 feet
Elevation difference: 1,144 feet	**Best lenses:** 35mm to 125mm

Directions: From the PA 33/PA 512 interchange south of Wind Gap, take PA 512 east through Wind Gap for 1.3 miles, turning right to continue along PA 512 toward the towns of Pen Argyl and Bangor. In Bangor, turn left onto PA 191 north toward Stroudsburg. Be careful to follow the PA 191 signs. After 5.3 miles, look for a large, five-car parking area on the left just shy of the mountaintop. GPS coordinates: 40° 56.177'N, 75° 11.732'W

Wolf Rocks is sort of the odd duck of mountain views. Although offi-
cially a ledge, it's really more of a pimple on the Pocono Plateau's flat
expanse. Blue Mountain, now Kittatinny Mountain, is a sharp-topped ridge
for almost its entire 270-mile length. East of Wind Gap, however, the
ridgetop slowly widens into a feature called the Little Offset. Still pushing
1,500 feet of elevation, the ridge has lost its sharp spine, replaced by a 7-
mile-long by 2-mile-tall S-shaped fold. Wolf Rocks happens to be a small,
rocky knob on this otherwise flat-topped ridge. As a result, the middle-
ground views are of trees, with valley views difficult to see, although this is
a nice summer sunset spot.

From the parking area, exit between two large boulders, one of which has a
white Appalachian Trail (AT) blaze. The AT is a wide, rock-strewn woods road
that makes a steady climb to crest Kittatinny Mountain. At .5 mile, a footpath
to the right leads to a campsite with a narrow view of I-80 to the north. It's
here that the AT narrows to a nice footpath where you can set a brisk pace.

The AT becomes a woods road again at .8 mile, where it turns right.
Shortly after, it makes another sharp right, marked by a double blaze. An
adjoining trail is curbed off. When you come to a power line cut at 1.6
miles, make a hard left just after reentering the trees. The trail climbs
slightly and becomes progressively rockier, until at 1.8 miles you climb up a
small boulder fall to follow the white blazes along the top of an exposed
rock ridge. This is classic AT hiking, as your boots don't touch soil much, if
any, all the way to the view, which is found at 1.9 miles.

Wolf Rocks is a fine north-facing ledge marking the maximum southern
extent of the Wisconsin Ice Sheet 10,000 years ago. Rocks making up the
ledge are conveniently stepped to form comfortable benches, so a picnic

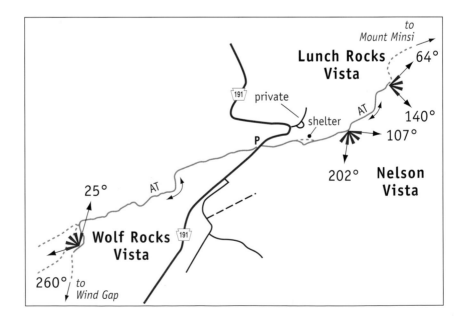

lunch is certainly in order. If you explore the length of the rock exposure, you'll find a black graffiti painted X and Z about 50 feet apart. In this case, X doesn't mark the best shooting spot, Z does. An exposed rock with a Celtic cross symbol (sort of a plus sign) has the best foreground. In summer, the sun will set north of the ridge, making this a superb sunset location. Fine images of moonset can also be made from here. In fact, moonset against the ethereal pink glow of earth shadow cast at sunrise is a perfect reason to hike 1.9 miles in the dark to get here.

Hike 76 **Nelson Vista and Lunch Rocks, Monroe County**

Nelson Vista

Type: ridge	**Field of view:** 107° to 202°
Rating: 5	**Relief:** 10 feet
GPS: 40° 56.283'N, 75° 10.983'W	**Elevation difference:** 816 feet
Faces: 154°	**Height:** 1,512 feet

Lunch Rocks

Type: ledge	**Field of view:** 64° to 140°
Rating: 2 or 3	**Relief:** 10 feet
GPS: 40° 56.583'N, 75° 10.617'W	**Elevation difference:** 725 feet
Faces: 80°	**Height:** 1,425 feet
Best times: early morning through midday	**Time:** 1 hour, 30 minutes
Difficulty: easy	**Elevation change:** 155 feet
Distance: 2.4 miles	**Best lenses:** 50mm to 200mm

Directions: From the PA 33/PA 512 interchange south of Wind Gap, take PA 512 east through Wind Gap for 1.3 miles, turning right to continue along PA 512 toward the towns of Pen Argyl and Bangor. In Bangor, turn left onto PA 191 north toward Stroudsburg. Be careful to follow the PA 191 signs. After 5.3 miles, look for a large, five-car parking area on the left just shy of the mountaintop. GPS coordinates: 40° 56.177'N, 75° 11.732'W

Nelson Vista is one of many hang glider launch sites. Although Lunch Rocks isn't much of a view, it's good enough to be worthy of extending this hike another mile. From the parking area, quickly and carefully cross PA 191, and follow the white-blazed Appalachian Trail (AT) northbound. After a little less than .4 mile, you come to an orange-blazed side trail called the Great Walk, which descends to private land. Shortly after, cross a phone-line right-of-way with a narrow southeast view. Beyond, a blue-blazed side trail branches to the left for Kirkwood Shelter, and then reconnects with the AT. Simply stay with the relatively level AT until you come to Nelson Vista at .7 mile.

Nelson Vista is a wide meadow. Small signs mark where the AT exits the woods and reenters for Lunch Rocks. Perhaps an old house lot from bygone days, this delightful location looks out upon two small farms and a large expanse of forest. The only thing marring the view is a coal-fired power plant at 120°. When breezes blow lightly from the east, pale blue gases can be seen spewing from the stack and settling into the valley below. Normally I like calm conditions for shooting, but a light westerly breeze makes all the difference in the world when shooting with the sun near the horizon. Enhancing the view is Minsi Lake, filling the middle ground toward the southwest.

From Nelson Vista, follow the AT back into the woods again. Look for a small, brown sign indicating north. The rocky AT descends slowly and meanders slightly before making a shallow climb. At 1.2 miles, you come to the 20-foot-wide ledge of Lunch Rocks. This small ledge has quite a bit of brush and several small trees in the foreground. Whether or not it's open will depend on trail maintenance. I've included it because when cut back, this location easily rates a 3, although when not, it's a mere 2. To your left is Indian Head, which is part of Mount Tammany in New Jersey. The cell and radio towers in view to the east actually sit at the top of Mount Minsi, where the AT begins its descent into Delaware Water Gap on this side of the river. A sweeping curve of I-80 on the New Jersey side can clearly be seen, along with the power plant visible from Nelson Vista.

Hike 77 Delaware Water Gap, Appalachian Trail, Monroe County

Lookout Rock

Type: cliff	Field of view: 6° to 106°
Rating: 4	Relief: 100 feet
GPS: 40° 58.113'N, 75° 8.113'W	Elevation difference: 430 feet
Faces: 50°	Height: 713 feet

Hahn View

Type: ridge	Field of view: 4° to 126°
Rating: 4+	Relief: 10 feet
GPS: 40° 57.756'N, 75° 7.633'W	Elevation difference: 1,007 feet
Faces: 65°	Height: 1,302 feet

Mount Minsi

Type: ridge	Field of view: 120° to 190°
Rating: 4	Relief: 5 feet
GPS: 40° 57.535'N, 75° 7.743'W	Elevation difference: 1,170 feet
Faces: 155°	Height: 1,465 feet
Best times: early morning through afternoon	Time: 3 hours
Difficulty: moderate	Elevation change: 1,324 feet
Distance: 5.3 miles	Best lenses: 20mm to 300mm

Directions: From I-80, take Exit 310 for PA 611 south at Delaware Water Gap. Whether you were heading southbound or northbound, carefully follow the signs for PA 611 south (Main Street), which will take you into the small town of Delaware Water Gap. Cross Cherry Valley Road/Oak Street, Shepard Avenue, and Church Lane, passing a post office on your right, and then turn right onto Mountain Road. After .1 mile, bear left onto Lake Road into a large parking area with a yellow gate at one end. GPS coordinates: 40° 58.799'N, 75° 8.512'W

This loop to the top of Mount Minsi and back is a popular hike in Delaware Water Gap, which is why the parking area is so large. From the parking area, walk past the gate up an old paved road with white blazes on the surrounding trees. This is the Appalachian Trail (AT). Within 100 yards or so, you come to a large pond filled with water lilies. This is Lake Lenape. Here the AT becomes a gravel road that divides. Bear left. At .3 mile, the AT turns left off the road onto a footpath, so turn left. The road will be your return route.

The AT hugs a series of ledges on the left, until at .5 mile you come to an overgrown overlook. This is Council Rock. When I was first here fifteen years ago, the view was really good, but now it's heavily overgrown with rhododendrons. The trail swings right away from the river and begins climbing around the head of a dry drainage. This happens again at a larger drainage at 1 mile. Shortly after, the trail returns to the gap's edge at 1.2 miles. Look here for a small sign in a tree indicating a left turn to a view. Turn left to reach a small headland called Lookout Rock in 15 yards.

This small area looks out upon the New Jersey side of the gap. From here, the colossal geological forces that squeezed and folded solid rock to create the Ridge and Valley Province are exposed across the river. Sedimentary rock layers are turned upward at a 50° angle and twisted and folded like taffy. Look for a massive rock exposure across the river, ending in a large headland to the upper right of Mount Tammany. This hundred-foot-thick layer of sandstone and conglomerate is part of the Shawangunk Formation, dating 430 million years old. On the New Jersey side, this formation is tilted upward almost 700 feet higher compared to the Pennsylvania side, with the fault's hinge point being a few miles northwest. Below is a raft launch and takeout area. On almost any summer day, you'll find the river filled with a

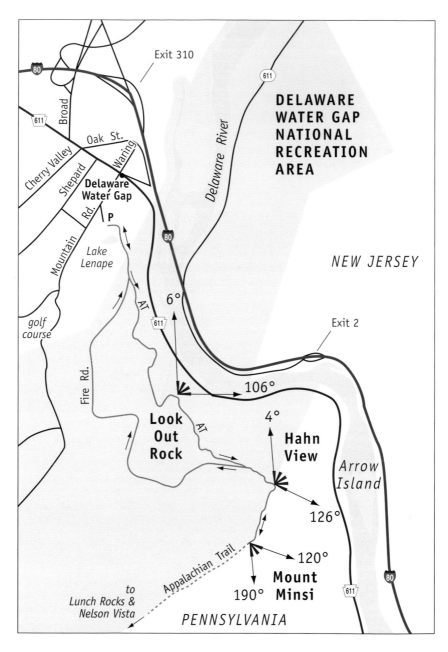

colorful array of rafts. During the height of day, any photograph will look unnatural with I-80 filling the bottom of the frame. In low light, however, you can use a long exposure to paint head- and taillights into an image.

Return to the AT and turn left, heading uphill. There will be a couple of switchbacks as the trail climbs steadily. Without much preamble, the real assault of Mount Minsi begins at 1.35 miles when you enter a rhododendron tunnel. The climb doesn't let up until you rejoin the Mount Minsi fire road at 1.8 miles. Turn left onto the wonderfully level fire road; then take an immediate right to stick with the AT, which makes a looping left to rejoin the road a few dozen yards later. Turn right onto the road and continue on to Hahn View, arriving at 2 miles.

Directly opposite, almost close enough to touch, is the exposed face of Mount Tammany, the top of which is 300 feet above you. To the left are the rhythmic undulations of the Ridge and Valley Province, and to the right is the expanse of Great Valley, which begins in the Blue Ridge of Virginia. In fall, this is a spectacular location, as the tree cover of Mount Tammany becomes a riot of color.

Continuing on, come to a communication tower and foundation for the old Mount Minsi fire tower at 2.3 miles. Look for a footpath to the left that takes you to an open grassy area, which is the Mount Minsi view. This wide tree gap looks out upon the heavily developed river south of the Water Gap. On your side is the town of Portland, and on the New Jersey side is Columbia. The power plant you see is 3 miles away. Looking deeper into New Jersey, you can see a long, sweeping curve created by I-80 as it speeds along toward New York City.

To complete the loop, return to Hahn View, and then where the AT bears right into the woods below it at 2.8 miles, bear left to follow the fire road. The road varies in quality from dirt to gravel and finally to something resembling a dry, rocky creekbed. Navigating this kind of terrain requires a certain inelegant walking technique. You can't walk stiff-legged as you would down a steep driveway, nor can you walk bent-kneed as on a flight of stairs. Instead, you need to set your feet slightly apart, bend your knees a little, and walk like Groucho Marx. It may look funny, but you can move very quickly over uneven ground this way. At 4.6 miles, the AT rejoins from your right near Lake Lenape. Continue straight on the road, returning to your car at 5.3 miles.

Hike 78 Tri State Rock and Cliff Park, Delaware Water Gap National Recreation Area

Tri State Rock

Type: cliff	**Field of view:** 98° to 248°
Rating: 5	**Relief:** 100 feet
GPS: 41° 17.420′N, 74° 50.089′W	**Elevation difference:** 475 feet
Faces: 192°	**Height:** 841 feet
Cliff 1	
Type: cliff	**Field of view:** 64° to 192°
Rating: 5	**Relief:** 80 feet
GPS: 41° 17.576′N, 74° 49.972′W	**Elevation difference:** 522 feet
Faces: 112°	**Height:** 889 feet

Cliff 2

Type: cliff	**Field of view:** 50° to 153°
Rating: 5	**Relief:** 90 feet
GPS: 41° 17.884′N, 74° 49.766′W	**Elevation difference:** 600 feet
Faces: 110°	**Height:** 937 feet

Cliff 3

Type: cliff	**Field of view:** 80° to 220°
Rating: 5	**Relief:** 150 feet
GPS: 41° 18.013′N, 74° 49.623′W	**Elevation difference:** 577 feet
Faces: 140°	**Height:** 944 feet

Cliff Park

Type: cliff	**Field of view:** 62° to 216°
Rating: 5	**Relief:** 80 feet
GPS: 41° 18.193′N, 74° 49.432′W	**Elevation difference:** 537 feet
Faces: 154°	**Height:** 904 feet

Cliff 4

Type: cliff	**Field of view:** 60° to 150°
Rating: 5	**Relief:** 50 feet
GPS: 41° 18.503′N, 74° 49.085′W	**Elevation difference:** 573 feet
Faces: 100°	**Height:** 940 feet

The Knob

Type: ridge	**Field of view:** 344° to 90°
Rating: 2	**Relief:** 20 feet
GPS: 41° 19.086′N, 74° 48.491′W	**Elevation difference:** 453 feet
Faces: 53°	**Height:** 820 feet
Best times: sunrise through midmorning	**Time:** 3 hours
Difficulty: easy to moderate; several ups and downs	**Elevation change:** 700 feet
Distance: 6.8 miles	**Best lenses:** All
Faces: Southeasterly	

Directions: The parking area is near Raymondskill Falls, so keep an eye out for those signs. From the traffic light at Dingmans Ferry, the PA 739/US 209 intersection, take US 209 north for 4.9 miles to SR 2009. Turn left and proceed uphill for .4 mile to the first pullout on the right. There is room for two cars. The large parking lot for Raymondskill Falls is just a little farther along on the left. GPS coordinates: 41° 17.424′N, 74° 50.392′W

Grizzled Warrior. I love trees like this. Grizzled old junipers that have been beaten by storms always end up looking like Zen paintings or bonsai trees. They're lovely to play with from all angles. *Tachihara 4x5 field camera, 210mm Schneider Symmar-S f/5.6, polarizer, 2-stop graduate, 4x5 Ready Load holder, Kodak E100VS, f/32 @ 1/8 sec.*

A brief climb through young pines and a woods road stroll are all that's needed to experience a lovely sequence of cliffs hanging above the Delaware River a short distance south of Milford. Step over the dirt mound and ascend the steep woods road. (If you have to walk around a gate, you're at the wrong parking area.) Pine saplings intrude, but the walk is pleasant, and it smells nice too.

At .3 mile, you reach an intersection in an open area. The road ahead is toward Cliff Park and the Knob. Turning right will bring you to Tri State Rock. Turn right, and at the top of the rise, you'll come to a concrete slab of an old observation platform. Go over the slab and descend along a prominent footpath toward daylight to arrive at Tri State Rock at .5 mile. Tri State Rock has an old grizzled juniper at the point of the headland. The view faces the river and provides a good look at the opening of Raymondskill Creek valley. A distinct cliff edge sits below a loose rock slope, so don't get too close to the juniper tree. Instead, stick to the grass above and use it as a foreground. US 209 fills the middle distance and far-right edge of the frame. In twilight, long exposures will create flowing red and white lines of vehicle lights.

After a short stay, return to the main trail. Your total distance now is .7 mile. Turn right and begin climbing again. In about 500 feet, a side trail on your right leads to Cliff 1, which provides a nice east view of the river and New Jersey mountains. The obelisk on the farthest ridge marks New Jersey's high point at Kittatinny Mountain, about 9.1 miles away. US 209 is not visible from here, so this view appears more natural than the one from Tri State Rock. A silo and farm fields sit in the foreground, and the Delaware

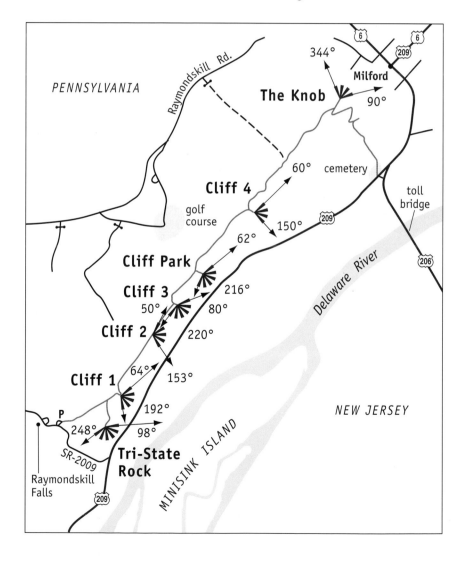

looks creeklike, as a smaller channel is on this side of Minisink Island. To the left, you can see the tollbridge at Milford.

From here to Cliff Park, the trail makes for good photography as well. Every tree is swaddled in lichen, and large, bizarrely shaped fungi cling to dead trees. If the light is not good for scenic views, then take some time to shoot the woods.

Come to another road junction at 1 mile and head straight. If daylight is on your right, you're heading the correct way. Continue along the rolling woods road to 1.2 miles and a second cliff exposure on the right. Cliff 2 is nearly 100 yards wide with several distinct openings and has a wide U-shape. If you look well to your left, you can make out your next destination, Cliff 3. There are several outstanding views of the farmlands on this side of the river. From here the woods road trail hugs the cliff for several yards before bearing away.

At 1.4 miles, you'll note that the ridge edge is higher than the trail, and a lot of daylight peeks through the trees. The woods road trail turns left and descends for just a few yards. Where the trail's left turn begins, turn right and plunge into the woods to get to Cliff 3. You've probably noticed that all the cliff exposures have a footpath running parallel to the edge. One of the fun things about scouting this hike was walking this path, brush busting as needed, for the entire 3 miles to the Knob. If you decide to do the same thing, take care how close you get to the edge.

Cliff 3 also affords an extensive series of exposures. On the left are a view of the head of Minisink Island and a more exposed look at the Milford bridge. After exploring, plunge back through the woods to the woods road trail and turn right.

The trail curves away from the cliff edges and descends slightly, encountering a junction at 1.5 miles. Continue ahead to another junction at 1.6 miles and turn right. You may find some old brown, blue, and red blazes or signs on trees above eye level, but I wouldn't count on these, as they are for an old trail system surrounding the Cliff Park golf course. Near 1.7 miles, the cliff edge comes closer to the trail and then moves away again. At 1.74 miles, you come to another road junction on the right, where a wide woods road descends toward the cliffs. Turn right and descend to Cliff Park, which is marked by several logs forming a rectangle on the ground. Your total travel distance now is 1.76 miles.

Cliff Park is a popular picnic spot for the nearby bed-and-breakfast located about half a mile behind you. This view is expansive, and again the Milford bridge sits to your left. From here you're now even with the head of Minisink Island, and the river is quite wide, nearly a quarter mile, as it splits around the island's head. Below you the farm fields are about half a mile wide. In April 1995, all of Minisink Island and the half mile of open ground below were underwater. You can find pictures of this flood event at the Dingmans Falls visitor center. Climb back from Cliff Park, and turn right onto the woods road trail.

Lunch and Camera. This is the perfect spot for a picnic. *Canon EOS Digital Rebel, Tokina 20–35, polarizer, 1-stop graduate, ISO100 setting, f/8 @ $^1/_{30}$ sec.*

The trail has a series of road junctions, all of which require that you keep daylight on your right. At 2.1 miles, you'll note exposures below and to your right. These cliffs are visible from the valley below, but unseen intervening ledges make getting to them problematic, if not dangerous, so make no effort to descend from the trail to these exposures. Instead, continue ahead to 2.3 miles to a prominent footpath on the right. Turn right and hike several yards to arrive at Cliff 4 in 2.37 miles. Here you'll find another wonderful view with just 50 feet of relief. Several small trees near the view's ledge could be overgrown in the coming years, restricting the number of setup positions.

In view to the left is the National Park Service guard shack, and just to the right of that is a small pond. The structure will make shooting wide landscapes a challenge. This view puts you north of Minisink Island, with the Milford bridge filling the middle distance. The view from here shows how the Delaware meanders between the straight cliffs you have been following since Tri State Rock. Return to the woods road trail and turn right.

You'll see more exposures on your right as you head toward The Knob, but again, they are not worth the effort to get to. The trail rises and falls twice before descending to a wide shelf or bench at 2.7 miles. From here to The Knob, there are no more views. At 3 miles, the trail sweeps right and descends, and then sweeps left again and becomes straight. Begin looking for a Moravian Star ahead of you at 3.3 miles, and you'll arrive at The Knob at 3.4 miles.

The Knob is a grassy knoll with low brush on the west side of Milford. It does provide a great view of Milford and the Delaware to the north as it meanders approaching town. A large cell tower at 40° breaks up the view. You can hear the hustle and bustle of everyday life as traffic sounds carry very well up the hill. I spent some time listening to Beethoven's "Ode to Joy" pealing out on church bells at the noon hour, with the refrain of "Joyful, Joyful, We Adore Thee" coming and going with the breeze. To return, reverse your route, arriving at your car at 6.8 miles.

By using two cars, you can shorten your hike by making it a point-to-point, parking one vehicle at the Milford Cemetery. Follow a gravel road from The Knob steeply downhill to the cemetery, arriving there at 4 miles. Then continue downhill through the cemetery, arriving at US 209 at 4.25 miles.

Hike 79 Pine Knob Tower, Lackawanna State Forest

Type: summit	**Elevation difference:** 390 feet
Rating: 5	**Height:** 2,260 feet
GPS: 41° 14.126'N, 75° 38.177'W	**Best times:** any time
Faces: Panoramic	**Difficulty:** easy; short stairway climb
Field of view: Panoramic	**Elevation change:** 20 feet
Relief: 20 feet	**Best lenses:** All

Directions: From the interchange of I-80 and PA 115 in Blakeslee, take PA 115 north for 6 miles, crossing PA 340. Turn right onto River Road (SR 2040) to head toward Thornhurst and Gouldsboro. In 5 miles, turn left onto Forest Road (SR 2016). Follow for 3.9 miles, and turn right onto gravel Pittston Road. A large Forest Service parking lot and trailhead for the Pinchot Trail mark the turn. Follow Pittston Road for 1.5 miles, and turn left onto Pine Hill Road, which dead-ends at the tower in .7 mile. GPS coordinates: 41° 14.126'N, 75° 38.177'W

The view from the tower is truly panoramic. The only issue is a cell tower at 277°. A wide mowed area at the tower's base helps keep foregrounds clean, but this is a bit of a party spot, so expect to have to remove trash from the brush in order to get the best photographs. Because it's only 24 miles away, you would think that you should be able to see Big Pocono State Park along an axis of 150°, but in fact you can't. Even though Pine Knob is high

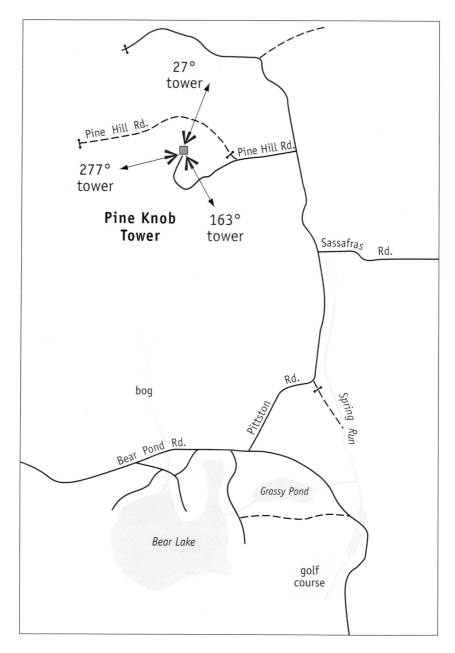

enough, a low hump at Tobyhanna is just tall enough to block the view of Big Pocono. The Pocono Plateau here is relatively flat, and the hills on it don't have enough elevation differential to see over the plateau's higher south edge. No matter, regardless of the geography, it's a grand view. If you shoot digital, try stitching together a full-circle panoramic image, which should be fun.

HIKERS PERCH on Pennsylvania's mountaintops for great view
of the state's unique topography and natural beauty. Thi
full-color hiking guide takes you to 79 of the most inspirin
outlooks across the commonwealth, offering detaile
descriptions of each hike, with maps and information o
distance, difficulty, elevation change, and highlights along th
way. Photographers will find tips on composition, exposures
unique perspectives, lighting, and gear.

SCOTT E. BROWN is an outdoor photographer who lives i
Horsham, Pennsylvania. His photographs have appeared i
numerous nature magazines and books. He is the author o
Pennsylvania Waterfalls: A Guide for Hikers & Photographers.

ISBN 978-0-8117-3439-4

STACKPOLE
BOOKS
www.stackpolebooks.com

$19.95 U.S.
Higher in Canada
Printed in China